Mel

The Last Los

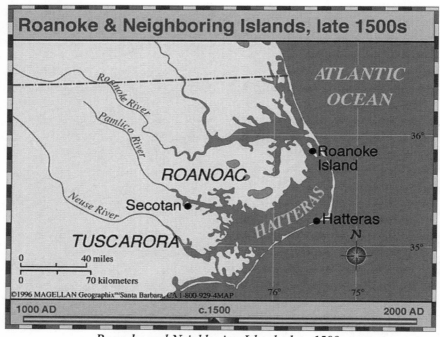

Roanoke and Neighboring Islands, late 1500s

Melungeons

The Last Lost Tribe in America

by
Elizabeth C. Hirschman

Mercer University Press • Macon, Georgia USA

ISBN 0-86554-920-6
ISBN 0-86554-861-7

MUP/H645
MUP/P245

The paper used in this publication meets the minimum requirements
of American National Standard for Information Sciences—
Permanence of Paper for Printed Library Materials, ANSI Z39.48-1984.

Library of Congress Cataloging-in-Publication Data

Hirschman, Elizabeth.
Melungeons : the last lost tribe in America /
Elizabeth C. Hirschman.— 1st ed.
pp. cm.
Includes bibliographical references and index.
ISBN 0-86554-920-6 (alk. paper) — ISBN 0-86554-861-7 (pbk. : alk. paper)
1. Melungeons--History. 2. Melungeons—Genealogy. I. Title.
E184.M44H57 2004
975'.0040509—dc22

6 7 8 9

2004014593

Contents

Foreword

Elizabeth Hirschman has written a thought-provoking and controversial book. In essence, Hirschman contends that the so-called "mystery people" of the American Southeast, the Melungeons, are but the tip of the iceberg of a much broader population of Semitic origins that fled from various regions of the world to America and, ultimately, to the Appalachians.

In her fascinating treatise, Hirschman provides evidence and documentation that supports her position that the European powers of the sixteenth and seventeenth centuries were settling the New World not with their own children, but instead with the children of those they considered ethnically and religiously undesirable. In a sense, Hirschman sees the Jewish Diaspora as having extended to the rugged peaks of Appalachia as surely as it extended to Eastern Europe, the Mediterranean, and Central Asia. She cites cultural and religious ties, oral tradition, physical appearances, and genetics as evidence of our nation's more diverse cultural heritage, and she presents her evidence with passion and conviction.

Whether one agrees or disagrees with Hirschman's premise, the reader will likely never look at Appalachia or our nation, or even the Diaspora in quite the same way.

N. Brent Kennedy

Preface and Acknowledgments

In December 1999, I was in the Atlanta airport waiting for a delayed flight back home to New Jersey. I wandered into a bookshop where I saw a book entitled *The Melungeons. Resurrection of a Proud People* by N. Brent Kennedy. I was intrigued by the title, because I had only heard the word "Melungeon" once before in my life. Growing up in Kingsport, Tennessee, my high school biology teacher had told us about a mysterious people who reportedly lived in the nearby Appalachian Mountains. They claimed to be Portuguese and were dark-skinned and dark-haired, with European features. Some researchers, our teacher told us, believed they might actually be the descendants of Sir Walter Raleigh's "Lost Colony" at Roanoke (1587)—but no one knew for sure. They had been living in the mountains for as long as anyone could remember. Our teacher said that he himself had never met any actual Melungeons, but that those who had met them said they were shy and preferred to keep to themselves.

Though fascinated by the teacher's descriptions, neither I nor my similarly dark-skinned, dark-haired, European-featured classmates went in search of Melungeons. We had no way of knowing at that time that we were those very same mysterious people he had been describing, a fact that had been carefully hidden from us by our parents and grandparents.

When I glanced at the pictures in Brent Kennedy's book and looked over the genealogies he had included, I realized I was seeing myself, my heritage, my ancestors, and my history. Indeed Brent and I turned out to be third cousins. (Cousinage, I came to learn, was very intense among the Melungeons who only married their own kind.)

It is difficult to verbalize how stunning a revelation this was to me personally and to the thousands of others who have recently learned that they share this same heritage. I had always been told I was "Scotch-Irish, English-Presbyterian" in ancestry and had always felt secure in my tidy WASP ethnicity. Through DNA testing and genealogical tracing, however, I now know that I am actually primarily of Spanish/Iberian descent with perhaps twenty percent Semitic ancestry and around sixteen percent Native American tossed in for good measure. Most of my ancestors were not Christians, but rather Spanish Jews and Muslims who had fled the Inquisition. What's more, I believe that some of my grandparents were aware of this and chose not to tell their children (my parents) or me, perhaps due to the rise of the Ku Klux Klan in the Southeast during the 1920s.

And so, I and thousands of others were left to discover our true ethnicity on our own—hit and miss, shock and dismay, denial and acceptance, we are all going through a journey of self-discovery. There are two photographs of my mother's family on the front cover of this book. They are a handsome family; they are a Melungeon family, and I want everyone, at long last, to know that.

My thanks to Brent Kennedy, Bennett Greenspan, Sara Froohman, Don and Teresa Panther-Yates, Abe Lavender, my mother Virginia Carter Caldwell, and my daughters Alix, Shannon, and Annie, for hanging in with me during this extraordinary journey. My deep appreciation to Bonnie Sage Ball and Jean Patterson Bible for their outstanding scholarship in first piecing together the historic fabric of Melungeon origins. And my gratitude to all my Sephardic, Muslim, and Native American ancestors for producing me, despite wars, inquisitions, and other hardships beyond my imagination.

Princeton, New Jersey   *Elizabeth Caldwell Hirschman*

Chapter 1

Melungeon Mythology—
Who Are We
and How Did We Get Here?

When I was in high school biology class in Kingsport, Tennessee, Mr. William Burns, our teacher, told us about a mysterious people who lived in the nearby Appalachian Mountains. He said they were called "Melungeons" and belonged to none of the "races" with which we in the South were familiar, that is, they weren't white people, they weren't Negroes and they weren't Indians. "Who are they?" we asked, "What do they look like and where did they come from?"

Mr. Burns told us that few local residents had actually seen any real Melungeons, but the ones who had, said they were slender, had long, straight, black hair, coal-black eyes and brown skin. They had faces "like white people," except much darker in color. They supported themselves by hunting, herding, fishing, and farming in their remote hills; they spoke an unusual language; they kept to themselves and it was best not to bother them. Mr. Burns told us, "It's believed they may be descended from the Lost Colony at Roanoke, Virginia in 1587, but no one knows for sure. They don't even know themselves."

In my mind's eye, I pictured these strange, exotic and frightening people: I saw them as dark and brooding, with bony faces and lank, wild hair, living down winding dirt roads in desolate cabins. Little did I imagine then that many decades later their identity would be discovered, and I would learn that I was one of them. In this book I will present evidence from multiple sources which affirmatively identifies who the Melungeons are and reveals the several sources from which they sprang. I will also provide material suggesting that two very famous Americans—Daniel Boone and Abraham Lincoln—were of Melungeon descent and, further, that many of the earliest colonists in the eastern portion of the United States were Melungeon as well. If you agree with my analysis of this evidence you will find yourself, as I did, reassessing much of what you were taught and believed about colonial American history.

These following five photographs show the diversity of Melungeon appearances in the present day.

Donald Panther-Yates

Emma Wampler Kennedy

Shannon and Annie Hirschman

Virginia Carter

Wayne Winkler

Several substantive research works have been written about the Melungeons since 1969, each building upon the others to identify their origins. Among the most popular and well-documented theories discussed are (1) that Melungeons are survivors of Sir Walter Raleigh's "Lost Colony" of Roanoke, Virginia; (2) that Melungeons are descendants of the ancient Carthaginians; (3) that Melungeons are remnants of the Lost Tribes of Israel; and (4) that Melungeons are the descendants of shipwrecked Moors, Portuguese, and Turks. Let's consider what earlier authors have had to say about these four possibilities.

Melungeons Are the Survivors of the Roanoke Lost Colony (Bonnie Ball, 1969ff.)

Roanoke Island

The first [English] settlement [in the New World was founded] on Roanoke Island [North Carolina] in 1854 [*sic*; that is, 1584]. Officers of this settlement included the following men:
[Master] Philip Armadas
Arthur Barlow
John Wood
James Brownwich

Henry Greene
Benjamin Wood
Simon Ferdinando (believed to have been a Spanish spy)
Nicholas Petman
John Howes
William Greenville [Grenville?]

. . . .

[On the first trip back to England, they] took two Indians . . . Wan-
chese and Manteo. . . . (It is believed that two Englishmen were left
with the Indians as hostages [for the safe return of the two Indians].)
Manteo became a true friend of the English; he was born, and many of
his kindred continued to live, in the coast town of Croatoan. . . .

The second voyage to Roanoke Island . . . was made by Sir Richard
Grenville in 1685 [*sic*; 1585], from Plymouth, England. It had as
principle "Gentlemen in the Company":

Raymond M. Stuckey
_____ Bremige
_____ Vincent
John Clark.

. . . Grenville left fifteen Englishmen at Roanoke Island in 1585.
They were later attacked by Indians from towns called Se-co-ta, a-quas-
cog-c, and Das-a-mon-que-pe-uc. Two [Englishmen] were killed and
several others were wounded. They escaped to boats and fled toward
Hat-o-rask, where they met four companions who had been hunting for
oyster; all later departed. . . .

Sams believes that "they attempted in their frail craft to coast down
to Croatoan, where they knew they had friends, and perished by the
way." All that was ever found of them were the bones of one at
Roanoke Island, who had been slain by the "savages."

A fourth voyage, this one under the command of Captain John
White, arrived at Roanoke Island in July of 1587. In this party were 150
men. . . .

After Captain and his crew arrived, they walked to the north end of
the island, where a man named Ralph Lane, from an earlier voyage, had
built a fort and a number of houses. [They found that] the fort was
razed, and the houses were in a dilapidated condition. Captain White
and his party despaired of ever finding any of the fifteen men alive but
did find the bones of one of them.

White gave orders to repair the houses and build more as needed.
Then on the 28th of July, George Howe, one of Captain White's assis-
tants, was slain by Indians as he waded, unarmed, in shallow water,
catching crabs. White buried him, and two days later, on July 30th,

passed by Croatoan Island with Manteo on the way to visit Manteo's kin and renew old friendships. On the 18th of August, Eleanor Dare, the wife of Annanias Dare and daughter of Governor White, bore a daughter they named "Virginia." Virginia was the first English child born in the new world, and was named for the settlement.

Soon afterward, the little colony began to feel the need of supplies, but because of the existing war on the open seas with Spain, all were reluctant to make the voyage [to England]. Finally Governor White consented to go. The war, and especially the threatened invasion [against England] by the great Spanish armada, further delayed matters. The invasion was imminent, and an embargo was laid on all English shipping. Nevertheless, Sir Walter Raleigh succeeded in fitting out two ships for the colonists in Virginia, but they were attacked by Spanish cruisers and so badly damaged that they returned to England. Other attempts to send supplies to Virginia failed, and eventually all ships were diverted to oppose the great armada and save England. For that, the colony on Roanoke Island was lost forever.

The fifth and last voyage to Virginia was long delayed and beset by numerous disappointments. Raleigh eventually obtained a license from the queen [Elizabeth I] to send three ships in which a convenient number of passengers, pieces of furniture, and necessities were to be landed in Virginia. But the order was not obeyed. Rather, in contempt of the order by government officials opposed to it, White was denied the privilege of taking passengers or anything else in his original mandate; in the end nothing went except the captains, the crews, and their chests.

Thus both masters and sailors were forced to disregard the interests of their countrymen in Virginia. For a time they did little more than remember Roanoke Island, concentrating instead on seizing Spanish ships and spoils, a task which consumed so many months that summer was almost gone before they reached the Virginia coast. That fall the weather was to be stormy and foul.

At night fell on August 12, 1588, they laid anchor at Hat-o-rask [Hatteras]. They saw a great plume of smoke rising on Roanoke Island, near the place where they had left the colony. This smoke inspired them with hope that some [settlers] might still be there.

On the 16th two boats went ashore and cannons were fired at intervals in an effort to locate the settlers, but to no avail. On the morning of the 17th, several men prepared to go up to the Roanoke settlement by water, but a gale broke on the bar, and a dangerous sea almost destroyed their boat. Seven of the crew drowned.

Finally, after much persuasion by Captain Cook and Governor White, they put off again from Hat-o-rask with nineteen men in two boats; it was dark when they landed, and they found they had missed their destination. They saw a great fire burning to the north and rowed toward it; as they neared the place, they sounded a trumpet, and afterward played many familiar English tunes, calling out in a friendly manner. There was no answer.

At daybreak they again landed, went to the fire, and found only burning grass and decayed trees.

From there they traveled through some woods but, finding nothing, went back to their boats and rowed to the place where White had left the colony months before. . . . [T]hey saw Indian footprints in the sand. On the bank they found a tree on which was carved the letters CRO; this, they believed, signified the place where they would find their lost comrades.

Next they saw an inland area enclosed by a tall palisade of tree trunks arranged to make a fortress. On the main post of the palisade, five feet off the ground, "in fair capital letters," was carved the word "CROATOAN." There was nothing else—no cross, no distress signal, nothing. Then the party saw where chests had been buried and dug up, goods spoiled by rain and tossed around, maps and books badly torn and damaged, armor corroded and rusty.

Severe storms struck the area and the party left. One ship's captain refused to do more and sailed for England; another postponed the return voyage "until a more convenient season," but did not go back to Roanoke Island. Eventually all three ships left, and the Lost Colony, if it was still alive, was gone forever.[1]

---

[1]By permission of Bonnie Ball, this essay on "Roanoke Island" is excerpted from Bonnie Sage Ball, *The Melungeons [Notes on the Origin of a Race]*, rev. ed. (Johnson City TN: Overmountain Press, 1992) 4-9. Ball's first edition was *The Melungeons: Their Origin and Kin* (Haysi VA: B. S. Ball, 1969; "2nd ed.," 1970; "8th ed.," 1984). Ball's "authority"—to whom she refers and quotes—for her essay on Roanoke is Conway Whittle Sams, *The Conquest of Virginia: The First Attempt; Being an Account of Sir Walter Raleigh's Colony on Roanoke Island, Based on the Original Records, and Incidents in the Life of Raleigh* (Norfolk VA: Keyser-Doherty, 1924).

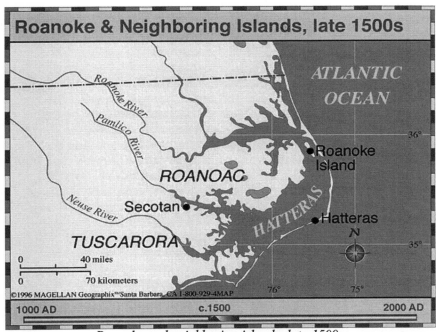

Roanoke and neighboring islands, late 1500s

In her essay on Roanoke Island, Ball includes a list of the Roanoke settlers "which safely arrived in Virginia [in 1587], and remained to inhabit there."

Men

John White (governor)
Roger Bailie (assistant)
Annanias Dare (assistant)
Christopher Cooper (assistant)
Thomas Stevens (assistant)
John Samson (assistant)
Dyonis Harvie (assistant)
Roger Pratt (assistant)
George Howe (assistant)
Simon Fernando (assistant)
Nicholas Johnson (assistant)
Thomas Warner (assistant)

Anthony Cage (assistant)
John Spendlove
John Hemmington
Edward Powell
Humfrey Newton
Thomas Gramme [Scot. "Graham"?]
John Gibbes
Richard Shaberdge (Shabedge)
John Tydway
William Browne
Michael Myllet
Richard Kemme

Richard Tauerner (Taverner)
Arnold Archard
Robert Wilkinson
Thomas Butler
Hugh Patterson
John Bridger
Grifen Jones (prob. Welsh)
John Burden
John Cheven
Thomas Smith
William Willes
John Brooke
Cuthbert White
John Bright
Clement Tayler
William Sole
John Cotsmur
John Jones (possibly Welsh)
Ambrose Viccars
Edmund English
Thomas Topan
William Lucas
John Wright
William Dutton
John Chapman
Hugh Tayler
Michael Bishop
Richard Tompkins
Henry Mylton
William Nicholes
John Nicols
Morris Allen

William Clement
Richard Wildye (Wilde)
John Wyles
George Martyn
Martyn Sutton
Mark Bennet
James Hynde
James Lasie (Lacy)
William Berde (Baird)
John Earnest
Thomas Harris
Thomas Hewit
Thomas Ellis
John Stilman
John Farre
Brian Wyles (possibly Willes)
Peter Little
Richard Berrye
Henry Berrye
Henry Johnson
John Starte
Richard Darige
William Waters
Robert Little
Lewes Wotton
Henry Rufoote
Charles Florrie
Thomas Harris
Thomas Scott
Henry Browne
Henry Payne (Paine)
John Borden

Women

Elyaner Dare (wife of Annanias)
Agnes Wood (probably single)
Elizabeth Glane (may be wife
    of Derby Glane, who deserted on
    Puerto Rico)
Alis Chapman (probably wife of John)
Elizabeth Viccars

Margery Harvie
Joyce Archard
Jane Pierce (probably single)
Audry Tappan [*sic*] (probably wife
    of Thomas Topan)
Margaret Lawrence (probably single)
Joan Warren (probably single)

Jane Mannering (probably single)   _____ Colman
Rose Payne (probably single)   Emme Merrimoth (probably single)

Boys and Children

John Sampson   Thomas Smart
Thomas Archard   Ambrose Viccars
George Howe (probably son of   William Wythers
     George Howe, killed by Indians)   John Prat
Robert Ellis   Thomas Humfrey

Children born in Virginia

Virginia Dare (daughter of Annanias and Eleanor)
_____ Harvie[2]

Commentary

Bonnie Ball's description of the founding and subsequent loss of the Roanoke colony is based upon popularized accounts, but it is quite possible that at least some of these colonists survived, joined the Croatoan tribe, and passed their genes forward to future generations. What I want to draw the reader's attention to, however, is not just the possibility of survival or death among these particular colonists, but rather their ethnic composition.

When forming a mental image of the "English colonists at Roanoke" most of us probably conjure up light-skinned, blue-eyed, blonde or fair-haired people, who look, well, English. But a glance at the list of colonists should suggest that this was not necessarily so. Names such as Philip Armadas, Annanias Dare, Dyonis Harvie, Simon Ferdinando, John Chever, William Lucas, Thomas Topan, John Farre, and Ambrose Viccars suggest a French/Mediterranean origin; and Richard and Henry Berrye carry a widely recognized Sephardic Jewish surname.

I propose that many, perhaps most, of these "English" colonists were not ethnically Anglo-Saxon, but rather Sephardic Jews, Moors, and French Huguenots who had immigrated to England for one or more gen-

---

[2]Revised listing from Ball, *The Melungeons*, 10-12. (Ball adapted the list from Sams, *The Conquest of Virginia*.)

erations to escape religious upheavals at home, and then continued onward to the Americas. This possibility receives additional support from Lee Miller's recent treatise on the Roanoke colony. In *Roanoke: Solving the Mystery of the Lost Colony*, Miller examines original letters, contracts, and other historic documents pertaining to Roanoke and its sponsor, Sir Walter Raleigh. From these, she learns that the "governor" of the colony, John White, was, in actuality, a watercolor artist who was friends with French artist Jacques Le Moyne, a Huguenot. Almost killed in the 1572 St. Bartholomew's Day massacre of 30,000 Protestants by French Catholics, Le Moyne fled to London as did young Sir Walter Raleigh, who was assisting the Huguenots. As Miller notes, many non-Catholic refugees fled to England from France during this time to escape death.[3]

Fifteen years later, 1587, Raleigh sponsored the colonization of Roanoke Island and named John White to govern it. White gathered together 115 men, women, and children, including his own pregnant daughter, Eleanor, her husband, Ananais Dare, another woman who had recently given birth and her husband, and another pregnant woman and her husband, nine other couples with small children; John Jones, a physician; William Browne, a goldsmith; Anthony Cage, a sheriff; Thomas Hewet, a lawyer; Thomas Harris, a professor at Cambridge University and Richard Wildye, a graduate of Oxford University—altogether an unlikely group to select for colonizing a remote, forested island, surrounded by Native Americans and subject to frequent hurricanes!

Obviously, we must ask ourselves why these people were chosen and why they agreed to go. Miller[4] supplies the answer—the Spanish Inquisition, aimed at killing or converting all Jews, Muslims, and Protestants, is expected to arrive in England by the following year; an Armada consisting of 130 ships and thousands of Spanish soldiers is being readied in Barcelona. Thus, White's unusual collection of colonists very likely felt that they were certainly doomed if they remained in England; their chances in the New World, though slim, were better.

Further suggesting that the Roanoke colonists were Jews, Muslims and/or Huguenots is the fact that their navigator, Simon Fernandez/Ferdi-

---

[3]Lee Miller, *Roanoke: Solving the Mystery of the Lost Colony* (repr.: New York: Penguin Books, 2002; repr.: New York: Arcade Pub., 2001; repr.: London: Pimlico, 2001; original: London: Jonathan Cape, 2000) esp. 25.

[4]Miller, *Roanoke: Solving the Mystery of the Lost Colony*, 159-60.

nando, was Portuguese and a former Barbary pirate[5] and that their onboard food stuffs were decidedly Mediterranean: rice, honey, currants, raisins, prunes, olives, beans, peas, salad oil and vinegar, turnip and parsnip seed, radishes, carrots, cucumbers, cabbage, lettuce, endive, onions, garlic, thyme, mustard, fennel, and anise, in addition to the English salted pork and beef, oatmeal, butter, and cheese.

Finally, prior expeditions to Roanoke Island financed by Raleigh in 1585 had included a man named Joachim Ganz, a metallurgist and specialist in gold and silver, from Prague. With this background and name, Ganz was in all likelihood a Sephardic Jew.

As we shall see before the end of this chapter, it was very likely a blend of Jewish, Muslim, and Huguenot religious castaways who became the Melungeons. This possibility, albeit set many centuries earlier, is discussed by Jean Patterson Bible, as in the excerpt below.

Members of a Lost Tribe of Israel?
(Jean Patterson Bible, 1975ff.)

Were Their Forebears Members of a Lost Tribe of Israel?

Could the Melungeons' forebears in America have been members of a Lost Tribe of Israel? . . . Occasionally one has heard old-timers who, when questioned, said they recalled grandparents or older relatives mentioning "something about a Lost Tribe." And most of the earlier writing about Melungeons suggests the idea merely as a possibility. As with some of the other more remote theories, any favorable evidence is strictly circumstantial, probably more of romantic interest, even to those propounding it, than from any real inclination on their part to believe in it.

Nevertheless, speculation on the Jewish angle did take on new life in the 1960s with the discovery of the inscribed Hebrew coins of the time of Bar Kokhba's rebellion against Rome in 132–134 AD, in the environs of Louisville, Hopkinsville, and Clay County, Kentucky, the finding of the Metcalf Stone in 1966, along with the announcement of Dr. Cyrus Gordon concerning the inscription on the Bat Creek Stone [found] near Fort Loudon in East Tennessee.

---

[5]As will be discussed shortly, these characteristics strongly suggest that Fernandez was either Jewish or Muslim.

Dr. Gordon says that the finding of the Hebrew coins was not considered of official significance at first because they were not professionally excavated, although they were identified by experts as authentic Bar Kokhba coins. But in the light of his newly revised concept of the Bat Creek Stone, consideration of the coins assumed a greater import, including the possibility that they supplied a missing link with the Lost Tribe [Cyrus Gordon, *Before Columbus* (New York: Crown Publishers, 1971) 175]. It was then that those interested in establishing a Melungeon connection with the Lost Tribe began to sit up and take notice.

The Metcalf Stone was so-named for its finder, Manfred Metcalf, who lived near Fort Benning, Georgia. Metcalf was seeking suitable slabs to use for a barbecue pit in the ruins of an old mill when he encountered a stone bearing such unusual and unrecognizable script that he promptly turned it over to Dr. Joseph B. Mahan, Jr., director of Education and Research at the nearby Columbus Museum of Arts and Crafts, Columbus, Georgia. . . .

. . . .

[A second stone, the Bat Creek Stone, has also been recovered which bears similar inscriptions.] This stone, now in the custody of the Smithsonian Institution, was excavated from under one of nine skeletons found in the [Indian burial] mound at Bat Creek [Tennessee] during a mound exploration program under the direction of Professor Cyrus Thomas and the field supervision of J. W. Emmert in 1885. It was accessioned into the museum in 1889 and the story of its discovery reported in the *Bureau of American Ethnology Twelfth Annual Report, 1890–1891*, published in 1894.

Dr. Gordon says that as early as 1964, a patent lawyer in Chicago, Henriette Mertz, had described the stone in her book, *The Dark Wine Sea*, and had stated that Thomas had published the text upside down, hence erroneously surmised it to be Cherokee script. According to her, the script was Phoenician (which contains Hebrew letter forms), but she made some errors in translation so her theory was discarded by experts [Gordon, *Before Columbus*, 182].

Later, Dr. Mahan, enclosing a photograph that the Smithsonian had prepared for him showing the Thomas one upside-down, notified Dr. Gordon that in this case the sequence of letters corresponded to those of the Canaanite alphabet. After a careful study of the inverted inscription, Dr. Gordon says its five letters are in the writing style of Canaan, the Israelites' "promised land," the fifth letter corresponding to the same style of writing as on the Hebrew coins of the Roman period. He translated the inscription to mean "for the land of Judah."

. . . .

For the armchair theorist, it is intriguing to ponder that a little less than 2,000 years ago, members of a Lost Tribe of Israel may have trekked an s-shaped route from today's site of Fort Benning, Georgia, to the present Fort Loudon, Tennessee, and from there to Kentucky. In the meantime, they either lost or buried some of the few pieces of the coin of the realm they had been able to smuggle out on leaving their homeland. And in the course of their travels, they thoughtfully took time to inscribe notes of their progress on stone. . . . Also, to connect them with the Melungeon story, some at least would have stayed in the region to intermarry with Indian women.

Such speculation is intriguing, that is, if the dreamer does not have to figure out what happened in the interim between 135 AD and 1974, or at what period in time and where they would have encountered Indians in the Southeast. Further surmise along that line might lead to one's wondering if the Jews were merely passing through or if they lived in the locality for some length of time.

For those who . . . are still fascinated with the Jewish angle, it seems to me that an even better case might be made for it by trying to establish a link between the early Melungeons and the Sephardic or Portuguese Jews. The time and travel element would lend it more plausibility.

With the Christian conquest of Spain in 1492, all Jews except those who agreed to renounce their faith were expelled from that country and from Portugal four years later. The Spanish and Portuguese Jews fled to North Africa, France, and Italy, and thence to Holland or England, others into Moslem kingdoms of the Mediterranean. Still others, or possibly some of those mentioned above, a little later came to South and North America and Mexico. [R. Brasch, *Mexico, A Country of Contrasts* (New York: David McKay Co., 1967) 128-31.]

The first one to arrive in Mexico was a shipbuilder with Cortes, who was awarded a land grant in 1521 for his participation in the conquest. Many others followed and even made names for themselves as civic leaders or in industry. But after the long arm of the Inquisition stretched out to include the New World, the majority of them slipped through churchly fingers to settle in Indian villages in remote parts of Mexico, where they intermarried with Indian women and concealed their identity. Until rather recently, their existence was virtually unknown. [Joan Dash, "Shephardim, A Modern Door to Fifteenth-Century Spain," *Américas* (October 1965): 10.]

The stumbling block here is that, although there are several fair-sized groups of such Jews in the United States today, there seems to be no evidence that any have ever been in territory even remotely near that of the Melungeons. . . .

Regrettably, it looks as if the "Lost Tribe" theory is so hedged by the historian's "perhaps," "probably," and "possibly," that it is hard to bridge the credibility gap. As far as a Melungeon connection is concerned, the Lost Tribe may have to stay lost for additional millennia.[6]

Commentary

As we shall soon see, Jean Patterson Bible's seemingly wistful speculations in 1975 have now become reasonable. New archaeological and anthropological evidence does support the presence of a substantial Sephardic Jewish and Moorish population in the southeastern United States. Dating from the mid-1500s and greatly expanded during the 1600s and 1700s, I propose that this set of Semitic émigrés formed the primary basis of the Melungeons. But there are two additional origin theories to consider, to which we now turn.

Are the Melungeons Carthaginians/Phoenicians?
(Jean Patterson Bible, 1975ff.)

The "Celebrated Melungeon Case"

It was in 1872 that a fledgling Chattanooga, Tennessee, lawyer based his case and won a lawsuit on the hitherto almost unheard-of theory that Melungeons were of Carthaginian or Phoenician origin. From this auspicious beginning, the young attorney, Lewis Shepherd, went on to become a judge and a leading member of the Chattanooga bar.

In 1915 Judge Shepherd published a collection of reminiscences of his legal experiences, entitled *Memoirs of Judge Lewis Shepherd*, which included the "Romantic Account of the Celebrated 'Melungeon' Case." In it, the judge recounts many of the details of the build-up, trial, and resolution of the lawsuit that has sometimes been dubbed the "Chattanooga Story" by those who sympathized with the plight of the Melungeons.

---

[6]By permission, this essay is excerpted from Jean Patterson Bible, *Melungeons Yesterday and Today* (6th prtg.: Signal Mountain TN: Mountain Press, n.d. [c1975]) 74-75, 79-80; Bible's footnotes are included here in brackets in the running text.

During the era in which it took place, the case was probably one of the most publicized of its kind where a decision was rendered favoring a minority group over a white prosecutor. The outcome, the awarding of an inheritance to the daughter of a Melungeon mother and a white father, hinged on Shepherd's successfully establishing his claim that his client was not of Negro blood, but was descended from the early Carthaginians. Had she been proved to have Negro blood, according to the then Tennessee law of miscegenation (Judge Shepherd defined it as the marriage of a white person with one of Negro blood to the sixth degree), the marriage of her parents would have been illegal, leaving her with no claim to her father's property.

The background of the strange true story that reads more like a romantic novel goes back to the early settlement of the Chattanooga area. A wealthy man from Virginia bought a large tract of land in Moccasin Bend. . . .

The fertile, river-bottom land soon became a rich and productive farm, so that by the time of the owner's death, he was able to leave each of his three sons a good farm apiece. Two of the brothers never married and, on their death, the surviving one inherited their estates. He rented the land, hired out his slaves, and went into business in Chattanooga.

In the meantime his widowed mother remarried and had three daughters by her second husband. Several years later, the surviving brother was stricken with a mental illness that left him temporarily deranged. By 1848, however, he was able to resume his normal schedule, including the management of his extensive holdings.

One of the tenants was an elderly Melungeon named Bolton who had served in the War of 1812, joining the army in South Carolina where he was living at the time. Bolton had a daughter "famed for her beauty, her grace of manner and modesty. She was a dark brunette. She had a suit of black hair, which was coveted by all the girls who knew her. Her form was petite, and yet, withal was so plump and so well developed as to make her an irresistibly charming young woman. . . . When she loosed her locks, they fell almost reaching the ground, and shone in the sunlight, or quivered like the glamour [*sic*] which the full moon throws on the placid water." [S. L. Shepherd, *Memoirs of Judge Lewis Shepherd* (Chattanooga TN, 1915) 83.]

The young man fell in love with her and the attraction was mutual. They planned to get married, but when the news reached his mother and half-sisters, they strenuously opposed the union, knowing that if it took place, they stood to lose all chance of becoming heirs to the property he had inherited. They notified the licensing clerk that if he issued the two a marriage license, they would file suit against him, claiming not only that the young man was mentally incompetent but that the girl had Negro blood and such a marriage would be illegal. The alarmed clerk was so impressed by their threats that he refused to grant the groom-to-be a license when he applied for one several days later.

Not to be outwitted, the young man persuaded two of his friends, Ab Carroll and John Cummings, to accompany him and the girl across the river to Dade County, Georgia, to serve as witnesses. The marriage license was purchased in Trenton, the Dade County seat, duly registered, and the ceremony was performed June 14, 1856, by a local squire at his Dade County home.

The couple returned to the groom's plantation and set up housekeeping. Their first child, a son, died in infancy, and the second, a daughter, was born in the latter part of 1858. When the mother died in childbirth, the bereaved husband was thrown into such a state of shock he never fully recovered. His mental condition was such that a guardian was appointed to look after him and manage his affairs.

In the meantime, the mother and half-sisters had not been idle. They either coerced or bribed "Aunt Betsy," the child's maternal aunt, into taking her far away and promising never to return. A little later, the aunt took the child, along with the family Bible containing the birth and marriage records, to a small place in Illinois, seventy-five miles from Cairo.

As time went on, the sad story was almost forgotten by the public. The insane man's guardian continued to manage his various properties until he had built up a fund of many thousand dollars for the estate.

But one person had not forgotten. A friend, Samuel Williams, had kept up with the child from the beginning by a secret arrangement with her "Aunt Betsy" to keep him informed as to her welfare.

The historic lawsuit was instituted in 1872 when the man's two surviving half-sisters and the children of the deceased half-sister brought suit in the chancery court attempting to surcharge and falsify the settlements of the guardianship by the guardian, Mr. Foust. He was charged with mismanagement of the estate, wasting its assets, lending large sums of money to poor risks, and taking inadequate security from them. In addition, they sought to make him account for assets supposed to be on hand.

The second feature of the suit was that Mr. Foust's ward was an incurable lunatic and that the complainants were heirs apparent who would certainly inherit the estate. They asked that the present guardianship be revoked and that the ward and his estate be turned over to them, promising to give bond and security that they would provide for his needs. Finally, they asked a decree adjudging them to be heirs apparent. And, for good measure, they also sued Mr. Williams and Col. John Divine, sureties on Mr. Foust's bond as guardian, in order to make good the hoped-for decree.

Now the time had come for Mr. Williams to produce the rightful heir to the estate and to protect her rights. Seeking a trustworthy and competent lawyer, he found that all the experienced ones were already involved in the suit on one side or the other. On the advice of a friend, he consulted Lewis Shepherd, a young attorney just starting out in his profession. Shepherd agreed to take the case, with Mr. Williams acting in the capacity of best friend of the young girl.

The suit they filed for the child came like a bolt out of the blue. They asked that she be adjudged the child and heir apparent of the deranged father, and that she be supported and educated out of his estate. The dismayed opposition promptly labeled the whole thing a "tissue of falsehoods and slanders . . . a fabrication of old man Williams, and that the girl was an impostor. They even denied her identity as the child of the crazed man, and also denied that he had ever been married to his alleged wife, and claimed that if he had gone through the form of marriage, it was void for numerous reasons, and the issue of such marriage was illegitimate." [*Memoirs of Judge Lewis Shepherd*, 85.]

At that time, young Shepherd produced his trump card, the daughter in person, then nearly fifteen years old. He had previously sent Mr. Williams to Illinois to bring her back to Chattanooga, along with the family Bible containing the birth and marriage records.

Proof of the marriage was not difficult to obtain as the magistrate who performed the ceremony and the two witnesses to it were still living. When asked how he remembered the exact date so well, one witness said that it was impressed on his mind because his wife had given birth to a baby girl that same evening, and the date and name were in the family Bible.

The record in the Bible carried to Illinois by "Aunt Betsy" verified the birth of the daughter and the date. As to the father's sanity, the judge ruled that marriage could not be questioned by anyone except the parties to the contract and could not be charged collaterally.

But the issue on which the real battle lines were drawn was the allegation that the marriage was void because the mother in the case had sufficient Negro blood that the ceremony could be not legally recognized, because of the Tennessee law against miscegenation.

The opposition brought in a number of old-time Negroes who testified under oath that the Boltons were kinky-headed Negroes, that "the whole bunch of them had kinky hair, just like a mulatto Negro." They also swore that: "Aunt Betsy" and the girl's mother had kinky hair, not knowing that the young girl was at that moment actually in Chattanooga.

The "kinky head" question was settled once and for all with a deposition taken from the girl at Mr. Williams's home. Asked to cut off a lock of her hair, and pin it to the deposition, "she reached up to her topknot and pulled out her old-fashioned tucking comb, and a monstrous mass of coal black hair, as straight as the hair of a horse's tail, fell down to the floor. It was about 4 feet long, and perfectly free of a kink or a tendency to curl. She exhibited with her depositions a fair sample of her magnificent suit of hair, which completely destroyed the depositions of the Negroes taken on the other side to prove that the Bolton people were Negroes." [*Memoirs of Judge Lewis Shepherd*, 89-90.]

By way of additional proof, Shepherd went back to the Melungeon tradition of Carthaginian ancestry in an exceedingly eloquent plea. In his account in the *Memoirs* of how he developed his defense based on the theory of Carthaginian descent, he [Shepherd] says

It was satisfactorily established in the proof that the family of this woman was in no way allied to, or connected with, the Negro race; that there was not a feature of herself or ancestry that was at all similar to the distinguishing characteristics or features of the Negro, except that they were of dark color, about the color of a mulatto. [Her family] had high foreheads; long, straight, black hair, high cheek bones, thin lips, small feet with high insteps and prominent Roman noses, while the features of the Negro and mulatto were exactly the reverse of these.

In truth, these people belonged to a peculiar race, which settled in East Tennessee at an early day and in the vernacular of the country, they were known as "Melungeons." It was proven by the tradition amongst these people that they were descendants of the ancient Carthagenians [*sic*]; they were Phoenicians, who, after Carthage was conquered by the Romans, and became a Roman province, emigrated across the Straits of Gibraltar and settled in Portugal. They lived there for many years and became quite numerous on the southern coast of Portugal, and from thence came the distinguished Venetian general, Othello, whom Shakespeare made immortal in his celebrated play, "The Moor of Venice." These were the same people who fought the Romans so bravely and heroically in the Punic wars, and whose women sacrificed their long black hair to the state to be plaited and twisted into cables with which to fasten their galleys and ships of war to the shore.

About the time of our Revolutionary War a considerable body of these people crossed the Atlantic and settled on the coast of South Carolina, near the North Carolina line, and they lived amongst the people of Carolina for a number of years. At length the people of Carolina began to suspect that they were mulattos or free Negroes, and denied them the privileges usually accorded to white people. They refused to associate with them on equal terms; and would not allow them to send their children to school with white children, and would only admit them to join their churches on the footing of Negroes.

South Carolina had a law taxing free Negroes so much per capita and a determined effort was made to collect this tax off them. But it was shown in evidence on the trial of this case that they always successfully resisted payment of this tax, as they proved they were not Negroes. Because of their treatment, they left South Carolina at an early date and wandered across the mountains to Hancock County, East Tennessee. . . . A few families of them drifted away from Hancock into the other counties of East Tennessee, and now and then into the mountainous section of Middle Tennessee. [*Memoirs of Judge Lewis Shepherd*, 87-88.][7]

As proof that Bolton had been consistently regarded as white since his arrival in Hamilton County, it was cited that the old man had been allowed to vote in all elections at a time when Negroes were not and also

---

[7]A list of possible Moorish/Sephardic South Carolina settlers is provided in appendix 3: "Purrysburgh Colony."

to testify in court when a Negro would have been regarded as incompetent to do so.

Moreover, Shepherd added that since the grandfather received a pension for serving in the War of 1812, he was legally considered white, because at the time he enlisted, neither Negroes nor mulattoes were looked on as soldiers and could serve only as teamsters or cooks.

. . . .

. . . [W]hen the final verdict was rendered, it was in favor of the girl. The court judged that she was the heir apparent of her father, entitled to be supported and educated out of his estate, and to inherit it on his death. Her guardian was instructed to pay for her education and maintenance, and to pay the young lawyer five thousand dollars for his services (a munificent sum for that time, especially for a beginner in law practice).

The true story of the young Melungeon girl not only had a storybook beginning, it also had a "lived happily ever afterward" ending. When Mr. Williams brought the girl back to Chattanooga, he had promised "Aunt Betsy" that he would bring her back to Chattanooga as soon as she could dispose of her belongings, a promise he carried out. In his memoirs, Judge Shepherd gives a summary of events following the trial.

When Mr. Williams got her back to Chattanooga, the girl was nearly fifteen years old. She knew nothing about the ways of the world. She was totally ignorant of the prevailing fashions of dress; she did not know what a corset was or how it was worn, whether over or under the dress. She had spent most of her life in the forests along the banks of the Mississippi, where she and her aunt had made their living by cultivating a small patch with hoes, and by cutting cord wood and selling it to the steamboats which plied up and down the river, and which used wood for fuel. She knew nothing whatever of the arts of fashionable women in making themselves attractive forms and figures by skillful lacing—she was simply an uncouth, an unsophisticated, unmadeup, natural girl from the backwoods; a girl withal, possessed of a strikingly beautiful face, and a figure which, by proper development and dress, was capable of being moulded into a form that would please the most fastidious.

She was very much like her mother, and possessed all the charms and grace she did, but they were undeveloped.

Mr. Williams took her to a milliner and had her provided with a wardrobe suitable to her changed surroundings. She very readily adapted herself to her new surroundings and her new life, out in the midst of civilization. She was kept at the Williams home and sent to school from there for about two years.

She had to be started at the very beginning, but being ambitious to get education, she studied hard and learned very rapidly, and in the short time of her schooldays got a very fair and practical education. She afterwards married her teacher, who was a splendid young man and became one of the leading men in the community, and managed his wife's affairs very successfully and added considerably to her fortune. At the time of his death, which occurred about twenty years ago, he was a prominent official in the county. [*Memoirs of Judge Lewis Shepherd*, 86.]

The echoes of the outcome of the "Celebrated Melungeon Case" reverberated throughout most of the Melungeon settlements in the Southeast. Undoubtedly it furnished a legal guidepost which affected decisions concerning Melungeons for many years afterward.[8]

Commentary

The Carthaginian story provides us with a second place of origin for the Melungeons that, as we shall see, can actually be supported by genetic, archaeological, anthropological, genealogical, and historic evidence. Dwelling in North Africa are tribes of fierce, nomadic tribesman, the Berbers, who in the year 710 AD crossed the Straits of Gibraltar with their Arab allies and conquered the Iberian Peninsula. Termed Moors, they remained in Iberia for 700 years, until the end of the fifteenth century. At that time the Reconquest of Spain by Catholic Christians and the subsequent Inquisition conducted against the Moslem Moors and Sephardic (Spanish) Jews, forced hundreds of thousands from both groups to immigrate throughout the Mediterranean and to Britain, Holland, and the Americas. As we will learn, some of the castaway Moors arrived in the southeastern United States from the 1500s through the 1700s. I propose that together with their comrades-in-persecution, the Spanish Jews, they became the Melungeons.

---

[8]Bible, *Melungeons Yesterday and Today*, 61-66; with permission from the author.

Attention should also be directed to the identity of the young Chattanooga attorney, Lewis Shepherd, who constructed the Carthaginian origin story seemingly out of thin air. Shepherd/Shepard is a common Melungeon surname, springing probably from a corruption of Sephard/Sepharad. Similarly, the given name *Lewis* is commonly associated with the Jewish tribal name Levi. Thus, I strongly suspect the reason Lewis Shepherd was knowledgeable of the Bolton girl's ethnic background was because it was the same as his own.

The Spanish, Portuguese, and English Tradition
(Jean Patterson Bible, 1975ff.)

The Spanish, Portuguese, and English Tradition

The most likely tradition of the Melungeon heritage, according to a majority of Melungeons and one shared by a number of early and later Tennessee historians, is that of Spanish and/or Portuguese mixed with Indian. The Indian background is usually attributed to the Cherokees, and occasionally to the Yuchis, a tribe virtually non-existent today, although there were a number of other tribes in the region at the time the Spanish or Portuguese are thought to have arrived.

One of the earliest records which might place one or both of the above nationalities . . . in East Tennessee during the sixteenth and seventeenth centuries is Abraham Wood's account of the travels of Needham and Arthur through the Trans-Allegheny territory in 1673. Tennessee historian, the late Samuel C. Williams . . . says that "from St. Augustine and Santa Elena, established farther north in 1567, the Spaniards were in intercourse with the Cherokee from an early date. They were in the gold regions of the southern Alleghenies in 1654. Artifacts found in very recent (1919) explorations of Indian mounds on the Little Tennessee demonstrate such early commerce." [Samuel C. Williams, *Early Travels in the Tennessee Country* (Johnson City TN: Watauga Press, 1928) 29-30.]

Wood was an explorer with a trading post near what is now Petersburg, Virginia, at a time when the Virginia colonists were beginning to show an interest in exploring the unknown territory beyond the Appalachians. He was one of the "Two Hundred Gent" employed by Gov. Berkeley to attempt to discover lands that "are of great hope for the riches of the mountains and probabilities of finding a passage to the South Sea." [Williams, *Early Travels in the Tennessee Country*, 17.]

On about April 10, 1673, Wood sent James Needham, a young Englishman from southern Carolina along with Gabriel Arthur, "who was probably an indentured servant of Wood," and eight Indians on a journey which began at Wood's post and ended in the first discovery of the Valley of the Tennessee and the domain of the Over Hill Cherokees by Englishmen.

Wood's account, as related to him by Needham and written to his friend, John Richards, treasurer of the Lords Proprietor of Carolina in London, describes the voyage down what is today the Little Tennessee [River].

> Eight days journey down this river, lives a white people which have long beardes and whiskers and weares clothing, and on some of ye other rivers lives a hairey people. Not many yeares since ye Tomahittans sent twenty men laden with beavor to ye white people: they killed tenn of them and put ye other tenn in irons, two of which tenn escaped and one of them came with one of my men to my plantation. As ye will understand after a small time of rest one of my men returns with his horse, ye Appomatock Indian and twelve Tomahittans, eight men and foure women. One of these eight is hee which hath been a prisoner of ye white people . . . ye prisoner relates that ye white people have a bell which is six foot over which they ring morning and evening and att that time a great number of people congregate togather and talkes he knows not what. [Williams, *Early Travels in the Tennessee Country*, 28-29.]

. . . [Williams] adds that the "white people which have long beardes and weares clothing" are Spaniards, as are the "hairey people." He observes that this corroborates the ancient Cherokee tradition of a "white race" in Tennessee as mentioned by Haywood in his *Natural and Aboriginal History of Tennessee* (pp. 234-37), "as well as circumstantial evidence of the fact that Needham and his party were among the Over Hill Cherokees." [Williams, *Early Travels in the Tennessee Country*, 24.] And almost certainly the bell tolling and congregating of many people indicates a Latin origin of some sort. . . .

[Thomas] Lewis and [Madeline] Kneberg [Lewis] comment in their book, *Tribes That Slumber*, . . . that the Yuchis were called by a number of different names, including the Tomahittans. . . . A little farther along, mention is made of the Needham expedition. "Beyond the Appalachians in eastern Tennessee, a large Indian town was visited in 1673 by an exploring party from Virginia. In the account of this visit, the people were called Tomahittans. . . . The explorers saw guns and brass kettles that had been stolen from the Spaniards in St. Augustine." [Thomas McDowell Nelson Lewis and Madeline D. Kneberg Lewis,

Tribes That Slumber: Indian Times in the Tennessee Region (Knoxville: University of Tennessee Press, 1958; 8th printing, 1986) 140-41.]

As to whether De Soto's route in Tennessee covered what was later known to be Melungeon territory, Dr. William Alderson, . . . states in an introduction in *Tennessee Historical Markers*, 1972, that

> The first known visit to Tennessee by white men was in 1540 by the Spanish explorer, Hernando de Soto. There is considerable dispute over his exact route, but the most widely accepted theory is that he came from northwestern North Carolina to the juncture of the Hiwassee River and Conasauga Creek, thence to the vicinity of Chattanooga, then back through the present states of Alabama and Mississippi and across the Mississippi River.

Mention of a later tradition backing the De Soto or Spanish connection with the Melungeons comes in a letter shown the writer by Miss Martha Collins from her late uncle, J. G. Rhea, who was born in Hancock County but was living in Griffin, Georgia, when the letter was written. Dated February 9, 1918, it was written in an old-fashioned script on rather yellowed paper and says that the Melungeons may be descendants of Spanish or Portuguese followers of De Soto when he came from Florida to Tennessee in his fruitless search for the fabled gold and silver. Some of them might have been sent to the East Tennessee mountains where they were either lost, captured, or befriended by the Indians in the region, intermarried with Indian women, and left descendants in what are today Rhea, Hancock, and Hawkins Counties, and adjoining counties in Virginia.

Mr. Rhea also spoke of Navarrh (Vardemon) Collins, who settled on Blackwater Creek and owned Vardy Springs. . . . Miss Collins says the spring was a health resort, [and] the name was later contracted to Varr, and eventually to Vardy, as the surrounding community is known today. The resort is long gone, but early in the twentieth century, the Presbyterians built a mission school, church, and teacher's residence there.

Miss Collins says that she and her family have also considered the theory that some of De Soto's men, daunted by the then unknown Mississippi [River] and its broad expanse, left their leader and made their way through or around Florida to the Carolinas, with whose coastline they were more familiar.

So from a traditional as well as historical background, there is a possibility well worth considering that some of these explorers . . . married Indian women and remained in the mountains, helping to compose a racial melange even before the family heads arrived from North

Carolina and Virginia who were later labeled "Melungeons." Some of their descendants may well have been Aswell's "scattered clots of shy mysterious people," or Sevier's "reddish-brown complexioned people in the high ridges of the Hancock and Rhea County mountains."

When the Spanish and Portuguese traditions are not considered together, the Portuguese seems to be the stronger, perhaps because of the large number of Melungeons themselves who have shared the belief and credited the legend as having been handed down from their forebears.

. . . One story relates that a band of shipwrecked sailors, marooned on the coast of the Carolinas, made their way gradually westward overland to the hills of East Tennessee, where they intermarried with Indian women.

Another slightly different version recalls that the Duke of Braganza sent a fleet across the Atlantic to take Cuba and Florida from Spain after Portugal's successful revolt against that country in 1665. If the attempt failed, the Portuguese were to continue up the coast northward from Florida and establish Portuguese colonies along the Atlantic coast. Apparently the fleet failed to reach its destination as it was never heard of again. The legendary shipwrecked sailors may have been part of the crew of one of these ships.

Still another variation of the theme is that the Melungeons are descended from a band of Christianized Portuguese Moors who fled to the New World to escape the horrors of the Inquisition's torture chambers. If we accept Judge [Lewis] Shepherd's explanation of the Carthaginian ancestry, such a connection seems reasonable. Carrying the Moorish idea further, Leo Zuber suggests that perhaps their dark coloring might also have come from ancestors who included tribesmen from the Sahara who settled in Portugal when the Moor Tarik conquered the Spanish peninsula. [Leo Zuber. "The Melungeons," manuscript no. G. 08. WPA Federal Writers' Guide, filed in McClung Historical Collection, Lawson McGhee Library, Knoxville TN, pp. 1-2.]

. . . .

Another strong supporter of the Portuguese theory was the late Mrs. Heiskell. The following is an excerpt from her article on the Melungeons in the *Arkansas Gazette*.

The Melungeons have a tradition of a Portuguese ship and a mutiny, with the successful mutineers beaching the vessel on the North Carolina coast, then their retreat toward the mountains, farther and farther away from the avenging law of man, going on where nature's barriers were their protection from a relentless foe.

. . . This strange people seem to have been forgotten by a century of civilization that has left its impress on everything else. They have some names that suggest the Portuguese ancestry, such as "Sylvester," but their surnames are anglicized to such a degree that to trace them to their originals would be impossible.

The Portuguese mutineers came to a region almost uninhabited, and because settlers were so few and scattered, the strangers were unmolested. Beyond the mountains . . . was the institution of slavery; when they went beyond their narrow confines they were in contact with the influence and prestige of the slaveholder. In all slaveholding communities all persons not white, or Indians, were classed as Negroes, and the name Melungeon was generally understood to mean a class of mixed-blooded but free Negroes. This they resented and insisted on their Portuguese ancestry. [As cited by Will T. Hale and Dixon L. Merritt, *A History of Tennessee and Tennesseans*, vol. 1 (Chicago and New York: Lewis Publishing Co., 1913) 180-81.]

Like Mrs. Heiskell, the late Mrs. John Trotwood Moore, a historian and former head of the Tennessee State Library, believed the Melungeons were of Spanish or Portuguese descent, and that they were in East Tennessee before the Revolution. She spoke of their original family names which she said soon disappeared with the arrival of the Scotch-Irish settlers in the mountains after the war. She, too, thought it likely that they had either taken the English names of the settlers or anglicized their Portuguese names. [Hale and Merritt, *A History of Tennessee and Tennesseans*, 184-85.]

This possibility has been noted by several students of Melungeon lore. Leo Zuber and both the Prices mention that names like Goins, Collins, and the occasionally heard Brogan might easily have been corrupted from Magoens, Colinso, or Braganza.

. . . .

Mr. Gibson's letter, quoted earlier, referring to the "dark-skinned people in the sand hill section of our country, reputed to be descended from Portuguese sailors," also adds legendary strength to the Portuguese angle. He writes, "I am confident that if the facts were known, this would be as historical as it is legendary."

Also the Hancock County census of 1880 lists a number of Melungeon names as Portuguese. However, a line has been drawn through the abbreviation, "Port.," indicating that perhaps the census-taker had changed his mind (or somebody else changed it for him) as to their nationality. It is noteworthy that the "Port," was omitted after Melungeon names farther down on the list.

. . . .

In my own family, those from Claiborne County who knew Melungeons always thought they were partly Portuguese. A cousin speaks of her great-great-uncle, a medical doctor living in that neighborhood, who often went into adjoining Hancock County to attend Melungeons there. She recalled that he usually considered them as Portuguese and had regarded them as white. My father spent a part of his childhood and most of his boyhood summers in Tazewell, clambering over the hills of Claiborne County, where he often encountered Melungeons. In later years, when I saw them in our community and questioned him, he said that he had always heard that they were Portuguese from the island of Minorca.[9]

Commentary

In this discussion, Jean Patterson Bible provides us with some very useful accounts of an early Spanish presence in the southeastern United States (that is, de Soto's foray in 1540) from which the Melungeons may be descended, and also several accounts of early Portuguese seamen stranded on the shores of this same area. What was unknown at the time of Bible's writing was that the Spanish also had a large colony off the coast of South Carolina from 1567 to 1587. Called Santa Elena, many of the Spanish settlers there were *conversos*, that is, Christianized Jews and Moors. What Bible was also unaware of is that Christianized Jews, who practiced Judaism in secret, often termed themselves *Portuguese* or *People of the Nation*. In our next account, a Melungeon descendant, N. Brent Kennedy, discusses these important points.

---

[9]Excerpted with permission from Bible, *Melungeons Yesterday and Today*, 93-98.

A Proposed Theory of Melungeon Origins
(N. Brent Kennedy with Robyn Vaughan Kennedy, 1994, 1997)

A Proposed Theory of Origins

To truly understand the origins of the Melungeons, it is essential that we review a number of key historical occurrences that undoubtedly influenced their ethnic makeup. Only by fully grasping the major political, social, religious, and cultural events of the centuries preceding their arrival on these shores can we gain a reasonably accurate profile of their so-called "ethnicity." . . .

In approximately 711 AD, Muslim armies left Morocco by boat and crossed the Strait of Gibraltar to the southern coast of Spain. Although they were no more than a few thousand hardy Arab and Berber soldiers, these brilliant warriors, driven by their recently acquired religious fervor, quickly and almost miraculously conquered Toledo and eventually most of the Iberian Peninsula. [Richard Fletcher, *Moorish Spain* (New York: Henry Holt & Co., 1992) 1.] Carrying out the will of God (Allah) and the prophet Mohammed, the dark-complexioned Arabs—who served as the officers and tacticians—and their equally dark but more ruddy-complexioned. . . . Berber soldiers (who made up eighty percent of the army's ranks) went about the business of making Spain an Islamic nation. Islam, incidentally, means simply "submission (to the will of God)," and its adherents join Christians and Jews as members of the "Abrahamic" religions. [See Warren Matthews, *Abraham Was Their Father* (Macon GA: Mercer University Press, 1981).]

The Muslim armies succeeded beyond their wildest imagination, effectively controlling most of the Iberian Peninsula for six hundred years. Even today, their influence on Spain's and Portugal's architecture, food, arts, music, and language is strongly evident. From exquisite architecture, to the efficient mining and smelting of precious metals, to the judicial processes, the Muslims taught their less-sophisticated Christian counterparts a new and more vibrant way of life. [Ahmad Y. Al-Hassan and Donald R. Hill, *Islamic Technology: An Illustrated History* (Cambridge and New York: Cambridge University Press, 1992).] . . .

These conquering warlords had two vulnerable points, however, that led ultimately to their fall from power during the time period of approximately 1150 through the late 1500s. First, they graciously tolerated the religion of their conquered foes. Being devout Muslims, they respected the God-given right to freely worship God (or "Yahweh" or "Allah" as the Jews or Arabs respectively referred to Him) in the manner of one's own choice. This right was extended to all "People of the Book." Christians and Jews were mentioned in the Holy Koran as being among God's people and therefore no attempt was made to interfere with their worship. So they were tolerant of the [Christian] Iberians . . . and this tolerance permitted the Iberians both to maintain a separate sense of identity and slowly but surely to rebuild their national fervor for reconquest of the homeland.

The second Achilles' heel of the conquering Muslims was the discrimination on the part of the Arab officers and national leadership toward their more numerous Berber compatriots. After conquering both Spain and Portugal, the Berbers were of little continued use to their Arab sponsors. The best lands were assigned to Arabs, not Berbers, and most real power rested with the Arab minority. Disgruntled, most Berbers took the least desirable, more mountainous lands in northern Spain and Portugal, and fairly duplicated the lives they had known in the Atlas Mountains of Morocco. . . .

Over the years, these Iberian mountaineers grew to resent the Arab power that had used them for the purpose of conquering these new lands. . . . Predictably, the Berbers became a thorn in the side of Moorish Spain, always rebelling, seldom following orders, and, along with the festering of Christianity, becoming a serious threat to Arab rule. So the combined flaws of religious toleration and bias against the Berbers led to the eventual collapse of Moorish Spain.

Like the celebrated fall of the Roman Empire, the collapse did not occur overnight. It took centuries, and the war was fought on many fronts by such renowned leaders as King Alphonso and his valiant warrior El Cid. Parts of Moorish Spain held out until the late 1400s, but by about 1200 AD most of the Islamic control was removed in the Reconquest. Nearly all Arab leadership fled the Iberian Peninsula, but some Arabs and nearly all Berbers remained behind. After all, these people had by this time been in Spain and Portugal for five hundred years or longer. They considered themselves Spanish or Portuguese, many had Iberian surnames and the lands of their origin were distant places they knew very little about. Some 500,000 of them, in fact, lived on the peninsula and were referred to by their native Iberian neighbors as "Mudejars" or "settled" Moors.

Following the Reconquest an uneasy truce was observed, during which time the Spanish and Portuguese Moors did their best to blend in with their Hispanic neighbors. In ever greater numbers they intermarried, converted to Christianity, adopted Spanish and Portuguese names, kept a low profile, and generally spoke Arabic or Berber only in the home. This worked for a while, but on 11 February 1502, under the

reign of King Ferdinand of Spain, the first throes of the Moorish arm
of the Spanish Inquisition began (a decade before, the Inquisition had
targeted the Jews and the Moors of Granada). With the encouragement
and blessing of the Catholic Church, forced baptisms of the Moors, or
"conversos" as both Muslim and Jewish converts were known, began.
The Inquisition quickly escalated until 1566, when simple political and
social pressure became brute force. By 1582, under King Phillip II,
thousands of Moors, including many conversos, were being exiled, with
a significant number garroted and burned at the stake. . . . The final
execution for heresy against the church did not occur until 1826. [Arthur
Griffiths, *In Spanish Prisons: Persecution and Punishment, 1478–1878*
(New York: Dorset Press, 1991) 113.]

. . . .
    Large numbers of Christianized Moriscoes were permitted to
emigrate to the Canary Islands and found final refuge there. [William
D. Phillips, Jr. and Carla Rahn Phillips, *The Worlds of Christopher
Columbus* (New York: Cambridge University Press, 1992).] Thousands
of others made their way to France, as well as Tunisia and Morocco in
North Africa. [Jan Read, *The Moors in Spain and Portugal* (Totawa NJ:
Rowman & Littlefield, 1974) 220-31.] And through those who went to
North Africa, vengeance—at least to some degree—was finally extracted
against the Spanish and Portuguese who had exiled them. In North
Africa the Berbers who had escaped the Inquisition often joined with
the Moorish and Turkish pirates on the Barbary (Berber) Coast to wreak
havoc on their former oppressors. These "Barbary pirates" attacked the
coasts of Southern Spain and Portugal with great ferocity.

. . . .
    Also during this time period, the Spanish and Portuguese were
laying claim to the New World. South America, the Caribbean, and
Florida were the focus of heavy Spanish and Portuguese colonization,
and historians have paid much attention to this vast effort. Less
attention, however, has been paid to the substantial settlements by the
Spanish in Georgia and the Carolinas. One such settlement, a colony
consisting of hundreds, if not thousands, of Iberian men, women, and
children was Santa Elena near present-day Beaufort, South Carolina.
Although most present-day Southeasterners know little, if anything,
about the Santa Elena colony, it provided the sixteenth-century Spanish
with a base for their operations in the Carolinas, Georgia, Alabama, and
Tennessee.

. . . .
    In 1566, Captain Juan Pardo, a Spanish officer most likely of
Portuguese origin, recruited some two hundred soldiers, probably from

the mountains of northern Spain and Portugal (that is, the Galician Mountains) and brought them to the Santa Elena colony. Pardo assigned these soldier-settlers to a series of four, or perhaps five, forts, in northern Georgia, western North Carolina, eastern Tennessee, or a combination thereof, depending on the interpretations of various scholars studying the question. . . .

In any event, Pardo left these soldiers with orders to hold the land for King Felipe and His Holiness the Pope, and then Pardo returned to Spain. Two and a half years later, he once again sailed to the Santa Elena colony, this time possibly bringing the wives and children of a number of these soldiers. Santa Elena, after all, was to be a permanent settlement and a permanent settlement required more than single male soldiers.

What is of great interest here is that if these soldiers were indeed recruited from either the northern Galician Mountains or southern Spain, then there is every likelihood that they and their families were of mixed Berber, Jewish, and Basque heritage. . . . [T]hey also would have been far easier recruits for resettlement in the New World than the so-called "native" Iberians, or those from more "pure" or wealthier families.

Indeed, in 1568, just one year after their immigration to Santa Elena, the Inquisition against the Moors went into high gear. It is quite possible that these soldiers and their families saw the writing on the wall and took advantage of an opportunity to leave before the going got even tougher. That young Christian men of Moorish origin were being recruited for New World service is well known. . . .

. . . .

Early Spanish and Portuguese New World settlers were of a varied ethnic mix not only in the southeast, but elsewhere. Marc Simmons in his fine book *The Last Conquistador*, a biography of sixteenth-century Spanish officer Don Juan de Onate [1500?–1624] who settled the American Southwest, relates much information relative to the ethnic makeup of Spain's New World settlers. [Marc Simmons, *The Last Conquistador: Juan de Onate and the Settling of the Far Southwest* (Norman: University of Oklahoma Press 1991).] For example, Onate himself was Basque and a number of his soldiers were Portuguese. Simmons also relates that, in times of peace, the Moors and Spanish often intermarried producing a sizable Iberian population of mixed heritage. Simmons points out another custom among these Iberian settlers: their tendency to name children for the cities or regions in Spain or Portugal from which they had migrated. This habit could be of great relevance in understanding Melungeon given names (for example, Navarrh Collins, Canara Mullins, Eulalia Nash, Elvas Hall). And in *The*

Jews of Spain, Jane S. Gerber postulates a Jewish tradition that is highly intriguing when coupled with the Melungeon insistence on being Portuguese:

> Even among themselves, the conversos in Lisbon, Madrid, or Seville referred to each other as "Portuguese," or "Men of the Nation," and the term "Portuguese" became synonymous with "Jew" or Judaizer" not only in Spain, but wherever these Portuguese New Christians went in western Europe. [Jane S. Gerber, *The Jews of Spain: A History of the Sephardic Experience* (New York: The Free Press/Macmillan, 1992.]

Regardless of their ethnic mix, these soldier-settlers, and likely later their families, were placed in fortifications throughout the (southeastern U.S.) hinterland, in advance of a proposed road to link Santa Elena with more distant settlements; and they never returned to Santa Elena proper.
. . .

. . . .
Historians have had no problem in accepting early Anglo survivors among the Indians. So why not Spanish or Portuguese? They certainly survived in the southwestern states, and—not being surrounded by Anglos in that more open region—were guaranteed the fortuitous maintenance of their names and culture. Conversely, any southeastern survivors were in a geographical chokehold, with melding, merging, blending in, their only hope of survival. . . .
. . . Evelyn McKinley Orr . . . has brought to my attention another possible source for the Melungeons, or at least a supplement to their population. Nineteenth century historian Henry Coppee wrote of the many Moors that escaped the Inquisition by crossing into Southern France and becoming French Huguenots:

> When the Moors were driven out, thousands took refuge in the south of France, who, abhorring the Roman Catholic persecutions, became Huguenots, and that of these many emigrated at a later date to South Carolina. . . . [Henry Coppee, *History of the Conquest of Spain by the Arab-Moors*, vol. 2 (Boston: Little, Brown, & Co., 1881) 445-46.]

. . . .
Dr. Chester DePratter [a University of South Carolina archaeologist] has discovered dozens of Portuguese intrusions into the Southeast, primarily between the years 1566 and 1575. Working on microfilm copies of the records of Spain's colonial archives of Seville, DePratter found dozens of cases of Spain's having sent Portuguese settlers to Florida and the Southeastern coast. While many such excursions consisted of but a

handful of sailors or navigators, others totaled as many as fifty and even one hundred Portuguese bound for the New World. [Archives of Seville (st. AGi) cards 11 and 12, 26 Jan. 1573, 13 July 1573, 86-5-19 and 256, pp. 35-36, and 139-1-12, and 321, pp. 5-7.][10]

Commentary

Brent Kennedy's discussion of the Melungeons' origins pulls together several diverse strands of Melungeon lore and unites them with new historic and archaeological documentation. Importantly, also, Kennedy exemplifies an upwelling of ethnic pride among Melungeon descendants.

It was Kennedy's book, *The Melungeons. The Resurrection of a Proud People*, that caught my eye at an airport bookstore in 1999. I bought it and spent the three-hour plane ride home scouring its pages, for you see, like Brent, I had grown up unaware that I was Melungeon. By comparing his genealogies with my own and looking at the photographs in his book, I discovered a large part of myself. Suddenly, my dark olive skin, brown eyes, dark hair, and Mediterranean "look" made sense. I launched into a quest to learn more about these mysterious people from which I sprang.

---

[10]Excerpted by permission from N. Brent Kennedy with Robyn Vaughan Kennedy, *The Melungeons. The Resurrection of a Proud People. An Untold Story of Ethnic Cleansing in America*, 2nd rev. and corr. ed. (Macon GA: Mercer University Press, 1997; [1]1994) 108-18, 126-30.

Chapter 2

DNA, Disease, and Demographics: The Keys to the Mystery

The work of Bonnie Ball, Jean Patterson Bible, and Brent Kennedy was central to the discovery of the actual origins of the Melungeons. But their arguments were based upon historical documents, eyewitness accounts, family traditions, and archaeology. Solid and reasonable and sound as these sources of evidence are, there will still be some naysayers who demand habeas corpus, that is, "Show me the body!"—the flesh, the blood, the genetic molecules that cannot be faked, covered up, or explained away. Remarkably enough, such evidence exists.

In 1969, two physical anthropologists, William Pollitzer and William Brown took skin color, hair form, and cephalic index measurements, together with gene frequencies in six blood group systems, from 177 Melungeons living in Hancock County, Tennessee, and Lee County, Virginia. Twenty-one years later, with DNA blood analysis much advanced, another physical anthropologist, James L. Guthrie, reanalyzed the Melungeon blood-sample data. He found that it was consistent with seven specific Mediterranean populations: Libya (Tripoli), the Canary Islands, Malta, Italy (Veneto/Venice), Italy (Trentino), Cypress (Troodes), and Spain (Gallicia). All of these populations are ones in which a substantial Sephardic Jewish/Moorish presence is documented. Because of the importance of Guthrie's research, I have included much of his original paper below.

Melungeons: Comparison of Gene Frequency Distributions to Those of Worldwide Populations
James L. Guthrie

Introduction

The origin of the Melungeons has been a puzzle for more than a hundred years. The orthodox view . . . is that they are a triracial hybrid of Europeans, Blacks, and Indians, and [some] claimed to recognize Cherokee, African, English, and Portuguese surnames in the group. However, Melungeons are reported to disclaim any Black heritage, considering themselves to be mainly of Portuguese descent. . . .

. . . .

Anthropologists Pollitzer and Brown . . . have published measurements of skin color, hair form, cephalic index, and gene frequencies in six blood group systems from 177 Melungeons of Hancock County, Tennessee and Lee County, Virginia. Their findings were in line with those expected of a Caucasoid population, with little evidence of Negroid or Amerindian influence. However, [despite this] they retained the traditional description of the Melungeons as a triracial hybrid. . . .

Survey of Worldwide Populations

What could be deduced about Melungeon origins if we had no preconceptions and used only published gene frequency distributions as the database? Worldwide data are available in the massive tabulations of A. E. Mourant [and others]. . . . These contain almost all blood group data published through 1975 (except haemoglobin data), calculated and presented in a standardized way.

For the present paper, all data in the ABO, MNSs, Rhesus, Duffy, and Haptoglobin systems were examined for values close to those of the Melungeons. Only populations with A_1 and A_2 differentiated were considered. The number of useful populations ranged from 773 in the Duffy system to 1,627 in the Rhesus system. Pollitzer and Brown included haemoglobin S (sickle cell) in their study, finding it absent in Melungeons, while present among Indians and English populations at levels of 1% and 8%, respectively. Its absence in Melungeons and the lack of haemoglobin data in Mourant resulted in omission of such data from the present study.

The Mean Measure of Divergence (MMD) of Melungeons from other populations was calculated for about 100 of the closer cases. . . . The method used here to compare data from only five blood groups is to be regarded only as a relatively simple but uniform device for estimating distances between pairs of populations. Each of the five systems was considered a single locus and was given equal weight. . . .

Table 1 lists MMD values for thirty-six populations in order of increasing distance from the Melungeon sample. Racial and regional designations are those of Mourant. MMD values corrected for sample size are tabulated in the final column. . . .

. . . .

There are 12 populations with corrected MMD values of 0.030 or less, and six of these do not differ significantly from the Melungeon sample at the 95% confidence level (p = 0.05). Except for the Minnesota sample of U.S. Whites, this set is from the Mediterranean region or the northwestern coast of Europe. Mourant's data give the impression that the people most like the Melungeons are in parts of Italy, but many populations are represented by data in only two or three blood systems. Also, data from France and Portugal are sparse and incomplete.

The next fifteen entries, with corrected MMD values up to 0.046, add populations from England, Wales, Germany, Greece, the Netherlands, Spain, France, Iceland, and Sicily. The small sample from Galicia is not significantly different from the Melungeons.

The final set of nine results shows the much greater MMD values for Southeastern Amerindians, American Blacks, and modern Turks. The Turks, represented by one small sample, would not be expected to resemble the people of ancient Anatolia to any great extent. Cyprus and Sardinia are included to show the degree to which their populations differ from those of Malta and Corsica.

It is recognized that small sample sizes, the availability of Melungeon data in only five systems, the uneven distributions of samples around the world, and changes in gene frequency distributions over time, limit the rigor of this treatment. Nevertheless, it seems clear that populations not significantly different from the Melungeons in these characteristics still exist, and they live in a relatively well defined part of the world. . . .

. . . .

. . . The Melungeon pattern . . . indicates a Caucasoid population. The Haptoglobin data narrow this somewhat, pointing to a European, and probably to a southern European or Mediterranean origin. A Black or Amerindian influence is counter-indicated. Values of Fy^a in the Duffy system tend to rule out much of an Amerindian component. The Melungeon value is closest to those of people now living in coastal Europe, north Africa, the Mediterranean Islands, the Levant, and to certain populations of Arabia, India, Africa, and eastern Europe.

In the Rhesus system, the Melungeon level of the cDe (R°) haplotype, a marker for Black African ancestry, is higher than for most European populations. This might argue for a slight Black American contribution to the Melungeons except that it is typical of many Mediterranean peoples through long contact with Africa.

In the ABO system, a distinctive feature of the Melungeons is their high level of A_2. It is second only to that of the Lapps and related groups of northern Scandinavia. The other center of high A_2 levels is southwest Asia, where certain populations of Cyprus, Iraq, Algeria, and Italy have percentages comparable to that of the Melungeons. The Melungeon value for the O gene is lower than average values for U.S. Whites and much lower than for Amerindians and U.S. Blacks, but is similar to values in certain populations of Cyprus, Crete, and Turkey.[1]

Thus, Guthrie's research indicates rather unequivocally that the Melungeons of Appalachia are derived from a Mediterranean base, and more specifically from populations having a Sephardic, Moorish and/or Arabic background.

Genetic Diseases among the Melungeons

As further evidence of Melungeon origins is the presence of several specifically Mediterranean genetic diseases within this population. Conveniently now, several internet sites outline several of these illnesses. Consider the following selection.

> *Bechet's Syndrome* is a relapsing, multisystem inflammatory disease in which there are oral/genital ulcers. There may be inflammation of the eyes, joints, blood vessels, central nervous system and

---

[1]Guthrie's original essay appeared in the *Tennessee Anthropologist* 15/1 (Spring 1990): 13-22; excerpted text, by permission, is from 13, 14, 15, and 18.

gastrointestinal tract involvement. Attacks last about a week to a month and reoccur spontaneously. Onset is usually between 20–30 years of age with symptoms occurring up to several years after the onset. Twice as many men as women are affected. There is a genetic predisposition with autoimmune mechanism and viral infection which may all play a part. Related disorders are Reiters Syndrome, Stevens Johnson Syndrome, and Ulcerative Colitis.

Joseph's Disease/Machado-Joseph's is a disorder of the central nervous system with slow degeneration of particular areas of the brain. Lurching gait, difficulty in speaking, muscle rigidity, impairment of eye movement are involved. Mental alertness and intellect are preserved. Joseph's disease is inherited through autosomal dominant mode of transmission, which means that it takes only one parent with the marker for you to have a 50% chance of inheriting the disease. Type I begins about age 20 years; Type II, about 30 years; and Type III, *Machado's*, after 40 years.

Familial Mediterrean Fever is a hereditary, genetically restricted disease commonly found among Jews originating from North African countries, Armenians, Turks and Arabs. Closely following the pattern of autosomal recessive inheritance (both parents must carry a recessive gene), FMF is recognized by two independent manifestations: (1) acute, short-lived painful, bouts of stomach pain (may be followed by diarrhea); pleuritis, an inflammation of the lining of the body cavities, and/or some of its internal organs, which in its acute stage may produce stabbing pain in the side or affected cavity, possible fever of 101-103 degrees, similar to gallbladder/kidney stone attacks/inflammation, and a short, dry cough and body pain similar to arthritis and fibromyalgia; and (2) nephropathic amyloidosis, which can lead to terminal renal failure even at a young age. In half of the people this disease appears before age ten. The gene for FMF is located on the short arm of chromosome 16, yet the exact nature of the disease remains unclear. Foggy-headedness (inability to think clearly) may also be a part of the symptoms because of inflammation of the brain lining which causes the brain to swell. Fatigue (severe) can also be a problem. Infertility and pregnancy loss in women with FMF is much more common than it is in the general population.

Sarcoidosis is a disorder which affects many body systems. . . . Onset is usually between 20 and 40 years [of age]. . . . Sarcoidosis is characterized by small round lesions of granulation tissue. . . . Symptoms may vary with the severity of the disease. Fever, weight loss, joint pain, with liver involvement and enlarged lymph nodes are common.

Cough and difficulty in breathing may occur. Skin disease marked by tender red nodules with fever and joint pain is a frequent manifestation.[2]

Thalassemia consists of a group of inherited diseases of the blood. About 100,000 babies worldwide are born with severe forms of the disease each year. Thalassemia occurs most frequently in people of Italian, Greek, Middle Eastern, Southern Asian, and African ancestry.
. . .

Thalassemia includes a number of different forms of anemia (red-blood-cell deficiency). The two main types are called alpha and beta thalassemias, depending on which part of an oxygen-carrying protein (called hemoglobin) is lacking in the red blood cells. . . .

Most children with thalassemia major appear healthy at birth, but during the first year or two of life they become pale, listless and fussy, and have a poor appetite. They grow slowly and often develop jaundice (yellowing of the skin).

Without treatment, the spleen, liver, and heart soon become greatly enlarged. Bones become thin and brittle; face bones become distorted, and children with thalassemia often look alike. Heart failure and infection are the leading causes of death among children with untreated thalassemia major.

Children with thalassemia intermedia may develop some of the same complications, though in most cases, the course of the disease is mild for the first two decades of life.[3]

Physical Abnormalities

Perhaps because of extensive intragroup marriage patterns (which are documented in chapter 5), Melungeons may exhibit several distinctive physical traits. Among these are the following.

Polydactylism. Children are born with more than five digits on feet and hands at a much higher rate among Melungeon descendants, than within the general population. For example, Brent Kennedy was born

---

[2]Excerpted from "The Melungeon Health Education and Support Network," a site tended by Nancy Sparks Morrison, as accessed on 21 June 2004 at <http://www.melungeonhealth.org>.

[3]Excerpted from the March of Dimes reference site, "Professionals and Researchers: Quick Reference and Fact Sheets: Thalassemia," as accessed on 21 June 2004 at <http://www.marchofdimes.com/printableArticles/681_1229.asp >.

with six fingers on each hand; my brother's son was born with six toes on one foot and six fingers on one hand. In both cases the extra digits were surgically removed shortly after birth.

Absence of "Wisdom" Teeth. Many persons in Melungeon populations are absent third molars (i.e., "wisdom teeth"). This, like polydactilism, is quite rare in the general population and is genetically linked. My mother, my three children, and I are all absent third molars.

"Shovel Teeth" (cynodont [teeth] or synodonty). Many Melungeon descendants have incisor teeth which exhibit an enamel ridge at the root. For example, Brent Kennedy, my brother, and my three children all exhibit this trait. Like the mouth (palatal) torus (below), concave incisors are linked to Native American and Inuit ancestry.

Palatal Torus. Melungeons, like Eskimos/Inuit, exhibit much higher than average incidence of torus, that is, bony bulges of projections on the roof of the mouth. My mother, brother, and two of my children all exhibit palatal tori.

Blue Nevis. This is a small (one- to three-inch) spot, which usually appears during the second decade of life in singular or multiple form. The spots are dark bluish/gray in color, slightly raised and usually found in the sacral area of the back, palms of the hands or soles of the feet. One of my daughters "grew" three Nevis spots at the age of ten, which are still visible on her lower back.

The Melungeon DNA Project

Once I discovered my Melungeon ancestry I became highly motivated (some, more accurately, might say obsessed) to track down all my known ancestors and have their DNA tested. I was very fortunate that the human genome had recently been successfully "mapped" and that commercial DNA laboratories were becoming available which would conduct paternal and maternal DNA testing at a reasonable cost. I contacted Bennett Greenspan at Family Tree DNA in Houston, Texas. He is a wonderful guy and has helped the Melungeon DNA Project from its inception.

To obtain the appropriate samples to determine my own ancestry, I posted queries on the GenForum Genealogy internet sites for each of the surnames I had in my genealogy. On each GenForum site I gave the specific lineage needed and offered to pay for the testing of a qualified donor. Fortunately, I was able to gather samples from all but a handful of my known ancestral lines.[4]

Concurrently, several other persons having Melungeon ancestry heard about the Project and joined us. Thus, the Melungeon DNA Project was born and now has approximately eighty-five donor participants. Several of the Y chromosome results are given in table 2. The lines to which I am directly related are starred with an asterisk. In terms of my own ancestry (using Y chromosome [male] lineage tracking), the majority of my male ancestors are in haplogroup R1b with scores centered in the Iberian Peninsula, that is, they were Spanish/Portuguese (and, I believe, Jewish or Muslim in religion). Three lines—Wolf, Blevins, and Nye—are Berber haplotype E3b, and one line—Perry—is Central Asian, haplotype G, but likely Jewish in religion, as Perry/Peary/Peery was and is a common Sephardic surname.

Among other Melungeon-descended donors to our project, largely the same pattern was found, with additional DNA input being found from Native Americans, Semites, Russian Askhenazi Levites, Subsaharan Africans, and Scandinavians.

---

[4]Those still missing are Greear, Bard, Davis, Hagey, Bickley, and Beeler.

Mean Measure of Divergence of Melungeons from Other Populations

Population	N_2 (range)	Uncorrected	Corrected
Libya (Tripoli)	138-2862	0.028±0.020	0.017±0.022*
Canary Islands	182-277	0.029±0.031	0.019±0.031*
Malta	117-164	0.030±0.025	0.018±0.025*
Portugal	302-4767	0.031±0.022	0.024±0.022
Italy (Veneto)	126-506	0.034±0.033	0.022±0.035
Ireland	>2000	0.035±0.052	0.029±0.052
Italy (Trentino)	149-383	0.036±0.011	0.026±0.012
Italy	>6000	0.036±0.026	0.030±0.026
Sweden	>5000	0.036±0.033	0.030±0.033
US Whites (Minnesota)	240-300	0.037±0.040	0.028±0.040
Libya (minus Fezzan)	218-3100	0.037±0.033	0.030±0.033
Britain	>4000	0.037±0.028	0.031±0.028
Cyprus (Troodos)	67	0.038±0.035	0.017±0.034*
Germany (Sacchsen)	>2500	0.038±0.026	0.031±0.026
Greece	148-3587	0.038±0.021	0.032±0.021
Netherlands	>1500	0.038±0.026	0.032±0.026
Spain (Galicia)	76-231	0.040±0.029	0.027±0.027*
Wales	115-1289	0.041±0.047	0.033±0.043
Corsica	132-1937	0.042±0.033	0.034±0.032
France	132-17,000	0.042±0.028	0.035±0.026
Spain	580-5200	0.042±0.037	0.036±0.037
U.S. Whites	>10,000	0.042±0.034	0.036±0.034
England	>3000	0.046±0.041	0.040±0.041
Iceland	135-2400	0.049±0.047	0.041±0.046
Sicily	107-2694	0.050±0.043	0.040±0.043
Northern Ireland	315-723	0.051±0.040	0.042±0.040
Finland (Häme)	627-970	0.053±0.072	0.046±0.084
Sardinia	644-2475	0.059±0.050	0.051±0.050
Cyprus	193-448	0.068±0.037	0.058±0.037
Turkey	108	0.068±0.062	0.053±0.062
Catawba (mixed)	104	0.121±0.091	0.108±0.088
US Blacks	>2500	0.195±0.099	0.189±0.098
Gullah (Blacks, SC, used by Pollitzer)	125-665	0.230±0.237	0.222±0.238
Seminole, Oklahoma	224	0.250±0.247	0.241±0.246
Cherokee	78	0.274±0.234	0.256±0.234
Seminole, Florida	381	0.316±0.252	0.308±0.252

*Means not significantly different at the 95% confidence level. SD is standard deviation of the five blood group values.[5]

---

[5]Table 1 from Guthrie, "Melungeons: Comparison of Gene Frequency," 16.

Table 2
Y-DNA Alleles for Melungeon DNA Project[6]

DYS#

Name	Haplo	393	390	19	391	385a	385b	426	388	439	389-1	392	389-2	458	459a	459b	455	454	447	437	448	449	464a	464b	464c
Locklear	o	13	22	14	10	13	14	11	14	11	12	11	28												
Sizemore	–	13	23	13	10	14	16	12	12	11	13	14	30												
Blevins*	–	13	23	13	10	17	18	11	12	12	13	11	30												
Blevins*	–	13	23	13	10	17	18	11	12	12	13	11	30												
Gordon	–	13	23	14	10	11	14	12	12	12	13	13	29	17	9	10	11	11	25	15	19	31	16	16	16
Carter*	–	13	23	14	10	11	15	12	12	12	13	13	29										16	16	
Bruce	–	13	23	14	11	11	12	12	12	11	14	13	31												
Chaffin*	–	13	23	14	11	11	14	12	12	12	13	13	29												
Wallen*	–	13	23	14	11	11	15	12	12	11	13	13	29												
Alexander	–	13	23	14	11	11	15	12	12	12	14	13	31												
Vaughan	–	13	23	14	12	10	13	12	12	11	13	13	30												
Skeen*	–	13	23	15	10	12	12	12	12	11	13	13	29												
Moore*	–	13	24	13	10	11	14	12	14	11	13	13	29												
Ney*	–	13	24	13	10	17	18	11	11	12	13	11	31												
Wolf*	–	13	24	13	10	17	18	11	12	13	13	11	30												
Campbell*	–	13	24	14	10	11	15	12	12	13	13	13	30												
Givens*	–	13	24	14	11	11	11	12	12	11	13	13	29												
Boone	–	13	24	14	11	11	13	12	12	11	13	13	29												
Wampler*	–	13	24	14	11	11	14	12	12	12	12	13	29												

	1	2	3	4	5	6	7	8	9	10	11	12	13	14	15	16	17	18	19	20	21	22	23	24	25
Caldwell*	13	24	14	11	11	14	12	12	12	13	13	29													
Panther-Yates	13	24	14	14	11	14	12	12	12	13	13	29	29												
Ramey	13	24	14	11	11	14	12	12	12	13	13	29													
Saylor*	13	24	14	11	11	14	12	12	12	13	13	29													
Harry*	13	24	14	11	11	14	12	12	12	13	13	29													
Woods	13	24	14	11	11	14	12	12	12	13	13	29													
Stewart	13	24	14	11	11	14	12	12	12	13	13	29		16	9	10	11	11	25	15	19	30	16	16	1
Stewart	13	24	14	11	11	14	12	12	12	13	13	30		17	9	10	11	11	25	15	19	29	15	16	1
Leslie*	13	24	14	11	11	14	12	12	14	13	13	29													
Johnson	13	24	14	11	11	14	12	14	14	13	13	29													
Berry*	13	24	14	11	11	15	12	12	12	13	12	30													
Kennedy*	13	24	14	11	11	15	12	12	12	13	13	29													
Gordon	13	24	14	11	11	15	12	12	12	13	13	29		17	9	10	11	11	25	15	18	30	16	16	1
Alexander	13	24	15	10	11	14	12	12	12	13	13	29		18	9	10	11	11	25	15	19	29	16	16	1
Christy*	13	24	15	10	11	15	12	12	11	13	13	29													
Cooper*	13	24	15	11	11	14	12	11	11	13	13	29													
Hale*	13	25	16	11	12	16	11	13	11	13	12	30													
Perry*	14	22	15	14	14	15	11	11	11	12	11	28													
Rogers	14	24	14	11	11	14	12	12	12	13	13	29													

[6]This table is available online at <www.melungeons.com>.

A Larger Issue

The presence of so many medical anomalies in such a relatively small population, especially those such as FMF which require the presence of *two* recessive genes, leads us to a larger issue: that of the persistence over an extended period of time of community cohesion so strong that out-marriage was rare. While one could argue that such "in-breeding" was the result of systematic exclusion from the surrounding "white" population, I will argue the converse in chapter 5. I will present genealogical material which shows a systematic, and I believe, quite purposeful pattern of selective mating by which Melungeon bloodlines were knowingly perpetuated.

In other words, persons of Melungeon heritage for many generations (that is, at least two and possibly four centuries) purposely sought out others of their kind as marriage partners. The biological result was the perpetuation of an almost "pure" Mediterranean type, complete with associated genotypic and phenotypic traits. The sociological result was the continuation of a secret community and an ethnic identity through decades of political, racial and cultural turbulence. To set the stage for these discussions we turn next in chapter 3 to a deeper look at the year 1492 and its aftermath.

Chapter 3

1492: A Most Propitious Year

The closing decade of the fifteenth century, and the year 1492 in particular, were momentous for world history. In close succession, three events occurred that were to have profound international implications and affect especially the people who would become "Melungeons." First, the last Muslim stronghold in Spain—Granada—fell to the Christian Reconquest on 1 January of the year. Moors across the Iberian Peninsula were faced with the necessity of either converting to Catholicism or leaving. Second, by the end of January 1492 the Spanish Inquisition was instituted. Directed primarily (at first) against Jews and Christian heretics, the Inquisition set out to enforce rigid adherence to Catholic precepts across the country. Third, on 3 August 1492 Christóbal Colón, an Italian sea captain, set sail across the Atlantic in three ships with ninety sailors on an expedition to find a western ocean passage to the Orient. His quest was financed by the Catholic monarchs Queen Isabella and Prince Ferdinand of Spain. Thus in this one fateful year we have set forth the three forces central to creating the Melungeons: Moors, Jews, and the New World.

Brent Kennedy's analysis (see chapter 1, above) has already provided us with an excellent overview of how these events coalesced into the arrival of the persons on American shores who would come to be called Melungeons. The purpose of this chapter is to provide some additional commentary and documentation concerning who, exactly, these people were. Where did they originate, what was their culture, and what did they take from the Old World to the New?

The Berbers

Let's first consider the Berbers, who, when they crossed the Straits of Gibraltar in 710 to conquer Spain for Islam, became known as Moors.

_____ *Kennedy*

Scott Collins

According to Brett and Fentress[1] the Berbers were, and remain, a group of loosely aligned tribes dwelling in Northern Africa. While some dwell high in the Atlas Mountains where they subsist as herdsmen, others such as the Taureg have operated cross-Saharan trade caravans since earliest times. Although each tribe has to some extent its own dialect and cosmology, Berbers as a whole have a decentralized social structure based upon kin groupings. They are fierce, resourceful warriors, who frequently feud with other tribes. They also are patriarchal and greatly value tribal autonomy. In many respects, their lifestyle resembles the Celtic culture of the Scotch-Irish, which may have made their cohabitation with members of this ethnic group in rural Appalachia comfortable and mutually appealing.[2]

---

[1]Michael Brett and Elizabeth Fentress, *The Berbers*, The Peoples of Africa (Oxford UK; Malden MA: Blackwell, 1997; repr. 2002).

[2]And the Berbers have to some extent Celtic forebears. Anthropologists have determined that early Celtic tribes settled in North Africa prior to emigrating to the British Isles.

Although the Berbers/Moors were ostensibly Muslim, Brett and Fentress wryly observe that this was for many a fragile religious commitment. Much like the quasi-Christianized Celts, the Berbers were at heart an animistic people, seeing spirits dwelling in the landscape, stars, moon, sun, animals, and vegetation.

Physically, they were—and are—distinctive in appearance. Typically Berbers are dark-skinned and dark-haired, have wiry, slender bodies, high cheekbones, long narrow heads with high foreheads and long slender noses. Very close phenotypic examples would be Melungeon descendants Scott Collins and _____ Kennedy (see photos previous page).

Berbers were and are nomadic people. In the past they relied little on agriculture and more on maintaining herds as part of a subsistence/transhumance lifestyle. They traded in Sub-Saharan slaves, salt, and gold. Traditional Berbers wore woolen plaid scarves beneath a black burnoose or hooded cape; they were excellent horsemen and migrated to the Iberian Peninsula in complete tribes.

The Berber aesthetic, as evidenced on pots, carpets, and jewelry, consists of complex geometric forms. Work within the tribe/clan is accomplished in a communal/mutual fashion, much as was common in early Celtic communities (including the Appalachian Scotch-Irish). The preferred location for their villages is in a remote, mountainous region. Their homes are built facing a central courtyard within a fortified enclosure. Brett and Fentress write, "Berber villages are regularly found on an almost inaccessible summit dominating a valley. . . . Defense and the desire for isolation from their neighbors must have predominated in the choice of site. . . . The migration into the mountains resulted from an acute sense of threat from neighbors as well as predatory nomadic tribes, and created an extremely high population density."[3]

The Berber household design was also distinctive, according to Brett and Fentress.[4] The only excavated example of an early medieval rural settlement comes from Spain. In Valencia, the castle or *hisn* of Uxo shows a number of extremely simple dwellings, one- or two-room houses clustered but not touching, and backed against the hillside where possible. In front, terraced open space took over the functions of a courtyard.

---

[3]Brett and Fentress, *The Berbers*, 245.
[4]Brett and Fentress, *The Berbers*, 237-38.

The Moors and Jews

The material from Brent Kennedy (chapter 1, above) well describes the Berber/Moorish invasion of the Iberian Peninsula in 710 and their subsequent presence there until the end of the 1400s. What I want to add to his discussion is some additional detail that will help our understanding of Melungeon origins. First, according to Fletcher,[5] we must recognize that the Berber/Moorish influx to Iberia during the eighth century, was *massive*—likely around 1,000,000 persons, if the entire entourage accompanying the 200,000 warriors is considered. This emigration was supplemented by *additional* large-scale arrivals of Berbers/Moors in 950 and 1170. Thus, by the 1400s, a sizable percentage, perhaps one in four, Iberians was of Berber/Moorish origin.

The Jews

A second important element in Iberian society was the *Jewish* community, which had been there since the first century AD.[6] According to Fletcher,[7] the Iberian Jews were engaged in widespread trade throughout the Mediterranean and generally enjoyed better treatment under Islamic rulers than Christian regimes. Thus, they were happy with the Moorish arrivals and quickly turned to assisting the new Islamic administration whenever possible. Together, the Jews and Moors of Iberia constructed an intellectual, economic, and aesthetic enterprise that was without parallel in the contemporaneous world. Mining, metalworking, ceramics, glass, woodworking, leatherworking, silk and woolen textiles, papermaking, bookmaking, architecture, and ivory carving all flourished in Moorish Spain, while medicine, mathematics, poetry, philosophy, astronomy, and navigation reached new heights of development.

---

[5]Richard A. Fletcher, *Moorish Spain* (repr.: Berkeley: University of California Press, October 1993; c1992).

[6]Recall the presence of first century AD Bar Kochba coins in Appalachia. Quite possibly, Iberian Sephardic Jews brought them in the 1500s.

[7]Fletcher, *Moorish Spain*.

The Inquisition

This flourishing of human creativity, however, came crashing to an end with the Christian Reconquest of the peninsula. The fall of the last Moorish stronghold of Granada in 1492 signaled the deathknell of this unrivaled period of Mediterranean cultural efflorescence—a span that had lasted 700 years. Concurrent with the Reconquest came the attempt by their most Catholic monarchs, Ferdinand and Isabella, to purify their kingdom of its Islamic and Jewish taint. As Roth keenly observes, the many Moorish and Judaic bathhouses and houses of worship—used to purify the body and the spirit—were quickly closed down and replaced with doctrinaire Christian "dirt and cathedrals."[8]

First Jews and then Muslims were subjected to heavy taxation and then forced to convert to Catholic Christianity. However, as Roth also notes, these *conversos* continued to practice their religions in private and—importantly for our Melungeon thesis—they continued to marry exclusively among themselves. The passage from Roth, below, describes this pattern clearly.

> The vast majority had accepted Christianity only to escape death, and remained at heart as Jewish as they had ever been. They took their children to church to be baptized, though they hastened to wash off the traces of the operation as soon as they returned home. They would go to a priest to be married, but they were not content with the ceremony and arranged another in the privacy of their houses afterwards. . . . Behind this outward sham, the recent converts remained for the most part nearly as Jewish as they had ever been. They kept all the traditional Hebraic ceremonies, in some cases down to the least details. For the most part, they married exclusively among themselves. They consorted familiarly with their former coreligionists, often continuing to live in the same quarter.
>
> Alternatively they would form religious associations with titularly Catholic objects, and under the patronage of some Catholic saint, use them as a cover for observing their ancestral rites. By descent, in belief, and largely in practice, they remained as they had been before the conversion. They were Jews in all but name, and Christians in nothing

---

[8]See Cecil Roth, *The Spanish Inquisition* (repr.: New York: W. W. Norton, 1964, 1996; c1937) 25.

but form. Moreover, they were able to transmit their point of view to their children, who . . . were as little sincere in their Christianity as their fathers had been. In Jewish life, they were known as *Anusim*, or the Forced Ones. But, as they went through the streets, the "pure-blooded" Spaniard would scowl after them. "Marrano," he would mutter, with expectoratory contempt. (The word is an old one meaning "swine," in both its literal and its figurative sense.)[9]

However, after 1492 the Inquisition began its work in earnest. Secret Judaizers were rooted out and subjected to brutal tortures and often death. Hundreds of thousands of conversos fled to southern France, Portugal, Italy, North Africa, and Turkey. By the mid-1500s Portugal, too, had begun its own Inquisition and waves upon waves of conversos fled from that country as well. Ironically, many of the Portuguese conversos crossed back into Spain—from which their ancestors had escaped fifty years earlier. The rearriving conversos called themselves "Portuguese," and it is likely in this way that those who became Melungeons gave their ancestry as "Portuguese."

At this point, the reader may be wondering why the Jews did not just leave Iberia? To which Cecil Roth replies:

It would be natural to wonder why the New Christians, persecuted as they were, persisted in remaining in the Peninsula. The reason was that it was universally realized that their first step, once they escaped, would be to revert to Judaism; and in consequence, over a large part of the period under discussion, it was forbidden, or at least made extremely difficult, for the suspects to leave the country. But notwithstanding this, there was in fact a constant stream of more or less surreptitious emigration; first to Italy, Turkey and the Mediterranean countries, a little later to Northern Europe—France, Germany, Holland, and across the North Sea to England. It was to Marrano fugitives that some of the most important Jewish communities of the world owed their origin in the first instance—those, for example, of Amsterdam, Hamburg, even London and New York. In all these centers and in many others, there were in the seventeenth and eighteenth centuries settlements of Spanish and Portuguese Jews (whose descendants in many cases still retain their identity), speaking those languages among themselves, perpetuating in the fogs of Northern Europe something of the stately traditions of Lisbon or of Madrid, and from time to time holding special services to

---

[9]Roth, *The Spanish Inquisition*, 26-27.

commemorate their kinsmen martyred in the latest *auto-da-fé*.[10] In some ancient synagogues, indeed, with a touching conservatism, a prayer is still offered up, on the most solemn occasion of the year, on behalf of co-religionists in peril at the hands of the Inquisition. . . .

The mental caliber of these fugitives may be gauged by the bare mention of the names of some of their descendants. Benjamin Disraeli, one of the most influential forces in British political life, Benedict Spinosa, father of modern philosophy, David Ricardo, founder of political economy, as well as his successor, William Nassau Senior, and Arthur Wing Pinero, one of the great figures in modern English drama, with David Belasco in America and Georges de Port-Riche in France, Benjamin N. Cardozo, justice of the Supreme Court of the United States . . . all these and many, many more were descended from families forced to migrate from Spain because of the Inquisition.[11]

By the mid-1500s, having hounded most of the Judaizers out of the country or burning them to death, the Inquisition turned its attention to the secret Muslims or Moriscos dwelling in Spain. In 1556 the Arabic language was forbidden; Moorish apparel had to be discarded and the baths which had been the pride of Moorish Spain were destroyed. Moors were rounded up and distributed in small groups around Spain, their houses and lands forfeited to the Crown. As Roth writes, "The political power of the Moriscos was thus broken, once and for all."[12]

Yet, many of the Moors, just as the converso Jews, continued to practice their religion in secret. The Spanish authorities responded in April 1609 by banishing all Moriscos. By 1615 between 300,000 and 3,000,000 Moriscoes had been forced from Spain, most fled to southern France, where they encountered those earlier Iberian exiles, the Jews.

Columbus and the New World

Thus, we have a situation in 1492 and for the next fifty or sixty years in which many hundreds of thousands of Spanish Jews and Muslims are

---

[10]*Auto-da-fé*, lit. "act of faith," designates the ceremony accompanying pronouncement of judgment by the Inquisition court and execution of sentence by civil authorities (routinely, the burning of a "heretic").

[11]Roth, *The Spanish Inquisition*, 146.

[12]Roth, *The Spanish Inquisition*, 158.

exiting (or being tossed, chased, or harried) out of Iberia with few options as to destination. Where to go? How about the New World? Roth writes:

> It is an undoubted fact that the discovery of America in 1492 was, to a large extent, a Marrano[13] enterprise. There is an old legend to the effect that Isabella the Catholic raised the money required by means of her court jewels; but as has been pointed out, it would be more accurate to substitute "Jews" for the last word.
>
> Be that as it may, there can be no doubt that Marranos had a great deal to do with the genesis of the expedition. It was one of them, Luis de Santangel, who commended the enterprise to the Catholic sovereigns, actually provided the money for it, and was rewarded by being the recipient of the first report of the discovery of the New World. His colleague and associate Gabriel Sanchez similarly played an important part. Indeed, the only high official concerned with the genesis of the expedition who was of "Old Christian" stock had a "New Christian" wife. Of the personnel of the expedition, many belonged to the same category—including Luis de Torres, baptized the day before they set sail, who was both the first European to set foot in the new land and the first to make use of tobacco; and Mestre Bernal, the ship's physician, who had not long before figured at [trial] on a charge of Judaizing.
>
> In the circumstances, it was not remarkable that crypto-Jews from Spain were eager to seize the opportunity of finding a fresh home and openings in the new continent, where not only was there opportunity for all, but above all the dreaded Inquisition was unknown. The emigration began at an early date, and there were even Marrano *conquistadors* in the little band which followed Cortes to conquer Mexico. But the optimistic hopes which impelled them to cross the Atlantic were ill-grounded, and it was not long before the nightmare of the Inquisition followed them. As early as 1515, a Marrano was brought back from Hispanola [West Indies] with his family to face trial at Seville. In 1528, the first Act of Faith [that is, Inquisition ceremony] was held in the New World, and two Spanish Marranos—including one of Cortes's old followers—were burned in Mexico City, while another was reconciled.
>
> In 1569–1570, Philip II of Spain secured the establishment in the city of Mexico of an independent tribunal of the Inquisition on the model of those which flourished in his European dominions, for the

---

[13]See Marrano = "swine," above. "Marrano," lit. "swine, pig" in Spanish, designates a (forcibly) Christianized Jew of medieval Spain (Iberia).

purpose of "freeing the land, which has become contaminated by Jews and heretics, especially of the Portuguese nation."[14]

Thus, it was small wonder that persons of Jewish or Moorish (Muslim) heritage in the early Spanish colonies would tend to be wary of practicing their religions openly. Further, it is also likely that they would choose to live at the edges of those settlements, as far from the center of political (and religious) authority, as possible.

And so, via Spanish expeditions, or through France, Holland, England, or Germany, or via Turkey, Italy, or Morocco there descended upon American shores from the mid-1500s through the 1700s a motley crew of Sephards and Moors. At different times, from different ports, possessing different means and abilities, they came to America. And some of them, it seems, made their way to the Appalachian Mountains.

---

[14]Roth, *The Spanish Inquisition*, 208-209.

Chapter 4

Rewriting the Past:
A New Origin Story

When I was a young girl growing up in Kingsport, Tennessee, my mother, Virginia Carter Caldwell, and Grandmother and Granddaddy Carter would take me every summer to the Chase Family Reunion. It was a rollicking event, often held at the Miller-Perry Elementary School playground in Sullivan County, Tennessee. About fifty to one hundred people would attend—Chases, Carters, Slaughters, Barkers, Perrys, Tates, Barnes, and Bonds of all ages—bound together by our common lineage to Samuel Chase of Maryland, a signer of the Constitution of the United States and a Supreme Court justice.

Grandfather Carter had at his home a small gray booklet called "The Genealogy of the Chase Family," which had first been compiled by J. M. Boyd and T. R. Chase in 1886 and then revised by Emery B. Chase in 1936. My grandfather, Daniel Edison Carter, revised and updated it once again in 1964. My name was in it, Marie Elizabeth Caldwell, together with that of my brother, John Richard Caldwell, Jr., our mother and father, our maternal grandparents, great-grandparents, cousins, and uncles and other Chase ancestors stretching back in a proud and unbroken line to a Mr. Samuel Chase who was born in London, married Catherine Davis, and died in London on 2 November 1722 at Brownstone Street, St. Giles Parish, London, England.

According to the genealogy, Samuel Chase and Catherine Davis Chase had a son named Richard who married a wealthy heiress, Margaret Francis Townley, in London. Because her father, Lord Jeremiah Townley, did not approve of the match, the couple immigrated to Somerset County, Maryland. The genealogy states that "Lord Townley died sometime between 1714 and 1750, leaving $6,000,000 in the bank of England, which has doubled six or seven times since then." Since Margaret was his only child, this would have left her quite a splendid inheritance!

According to the genealogy, Richard and Margaret had three sons: Richard, Jeremiah, and Walter. Walter was "our" ancestor. The booklet reports that Walter Chase first married a Lucy Barker, by whom he had a son, Richard, born 21 April 1767, who did not marry and died in Maryland. He also had a daughter named Annie, born 25 December 1768, who later married a George Haile.[1]

When Lucy Barker died, Walter remarried, to Sarah Haile on 7 April 1776. (Sarah's parents, I later learned, were George Haile, Sr. and Elizabeth Chaffin Haile.) Two children were born to this union: Jeremiah Townley Chase (born 22 July 1778), who married Nancy Perry[2] on 1 June 1800, and Walter Jr., born, rather oddly, a decade later, on 15 July 1788. Walter himself died in 1788, either shortly before or after his own son Walter Jr.'s birth.

According to the booklet, Sarah Haile Chase left Maryland the following year (1789), and with twenty-year-old Annie Chase, Jeremiah Townley Chase, age ten or eleven, and one-year-old Walter Jr., she traveled 600 miles over difficult roads and trails, into the barely settled wilderness tract of Jonesborough, Tennessee. Why, at the age of thirty-nine or forty, with one stepchild, a young son and an infant, would a woman whose husband's lineage implied direct access to great wealth and social position in London and Baltimore go trekking cross-country to Jonesborough, Tennessee? It makes no sense. Unless, of course, the lineage isn't what it purports to be.[3]

In the early 1980s, after the birth of my first child, proudly named *Alixandra Chase Hale* Hirschman, I went to see a prominent genealogist on Park Avenue in New York City to seek help in applying to the DAR. I presented her with my little gray Chase family genealogy booklet, sure I would be ushered into the DAR in short order.

But to my shock and surprise, the genealogist could find no evidence of a Walter Chase being the son of Richard Chase of Maryland, a man whose social prominence left his life quite well documented. Further,

---

[1]This George Haile was the brother of Walter's second wife, Sarah Haile.

[2]This Nancy Perry, as we shall soon see, was likely Jeremiah Townley Chase's first cousin.

[3]And as the astute reader has likely already noted, we were not even shown in the booklet to be related to *Maryland's* Samuel Chase (the signer of the Constitution) as our family tradition held, but rather to an *English* Samuel Chase!

"poor Walter," as the genealogist tagged him, sprang from none of the other Maryland Chases either—not Samuel, not Thomas, not Jeremiah Townley. The only record she could find for him was that a Walter *Perry* Chase did sign a loyalty oath (to the Revolutionary cause) and did marry a Sarah Haile, daughter of George Haile, in 1776.

Who was Walter Perry Chase? We will probably never know for sure. A search through the voluminous documentation of early Maryland settlers reveals no trace of him, save what is given above. However, there are clues. Interestingly, his name in the family genealogy is always given as Walter Chase, not Walter *Perry* Chase, as the few genuine historical documents list it. Jourdan (1996) in volume 5 of *Early Families of Southern Maryland* devotes a full twenty-five pages to settlers whose surnames were Pery, Perry, Perrie, Pere, Pearre, and Perrey. Many of these persons were *transported* to the early Maryland colony as servants or indentures, although some arrived as doctors or military officers. Perry (and its variants) was a very common Sephardic name and no doubt many of the Perrys arriving on Colonial Maryland shores were of Sephardic descent and limited economic means.

The Healle/Hail/Hale/Haile family into which Walter Perry Chase married was likely of Sephardic extraction, as was that of Sarah Hale's mother, Elizabeth Chafin.[4] Further, when Sarah Haile Chase arrived in Jonesborough, she found Hailes and Perrys from Maryland already there. Her stepdaughter, Annie Chase married a George Haile in Jonesborough; her son, Jeremiah Townley Chase, married a Nancy Perry in Jonesborough. And through subsequent research I learned that Joseph and Abraham Haile, two of Sarah Haile Chase's nephews, already were in Jonesborough at the time of her arrival there.

Thus I believe Walter Perry Chase was most likely just Walter *Perry*; perhaps he was an indentured servant for the Chase family who adopted their last name to ease his transition into colonial society. Perhaps he simply admired the prestige of the Chase family and decided to append its name to his own. We will likely never know for sure. But we do know that he was most probably not a Chase, but rather a Perry, by birth—an immigrant Sephardic Jew and not a WASP-to-the-manner-born.

---

[4]Recent DNA analyses have confirmed that the primary matches for these lineages are in Iberia. See <www.melungeons.com>.

Why the Perrys and Hailes Came to Jonesborough, or the Great Melungeon Migration

What could have possessed the Perrys, the Hailes, and the Chaffins—not to mention the Greenes, the Leslies, the Moores, Wallens, Browns, Berrys, Davises, Coopers, and Wolfes in my ancestry—to forsake their homes and lands in Maryland, Virginia, and South Carolina and travel over rugged and dangerous terrain to what in 1790 was essentially "the middle of nowhere" in the Appalachian Mountains?

The answer to this question lies in the history of the discovery of this particular "middle of nowhere." The area that is now southwestern Virginia, western North Carolina, eastern Tennessee, southern West Virginia, and southeastern Kentucky was once the Appalachian wilderness known only to Native American tribes, such as the Cherokee and Shawnee, and the converso remnants of Ferdinand de Soto's explorations in 1540 and Juan Pardo's expeditions in 1567. As we have seen, it is likely that these Spanish and Native Americans could have trekked through most of Appalachia from the mid-1500s to the mid-1700s largely unmolested, as the English, Germans, and Scotch-Irish had not yet arrived.[5]

On a trip to Appalachia in summer 2000, I purchased all available histories of the region. From these I learned that when the first "English" explorers did officially arrive, they were an interesting and multiethnic lot. In 1641, the citizens of Virginia petitioned their House of Burgesses for permission to explore west and south of the Appomattox River, and in March 1642 permission was granted. One of the citizens to whom the grant was made was *Major Abram Wood*. In 1654, Wood ventured across the Allegheny Mountains towards the Blue Ridge Mountains, discovering a river (New River) and a gap in the mountains (Wood's Gap). In 1671, a group of five Virginians revisited this same area and claimed it for Britain.

---

[5]And, as Miller (*Roanoke: Solving the Mystery of the Lost Colony*, 2000) correctly observes, they would have been traveling along a well-known Native American trading trail which extended from the South Carolina coast through the Yadkin area of North Carolina, across the mountains into eastern Tennessee and then south, terminating at present-day Augusta, Georgia.

No further explorations were made of the area until August 1716 when Governor Alexander Spotswood of Virginia and "several members of his staff left Williamsburg by coach and proceeded to Germania. At Germania this party was supplemented by a number of gentlemen, their retainers, a company of rangers and four Meherrin Indians—about fifty persons in all. On the 36th day out, being 5 September 1716, they scaled the Blue Ridge at Swift Run Gap, now in Augusta County (Va.)."[6]

Now we must supplement the historical record with some additional and significant information. Major Abram Wood was part of a large Sephardic family which had arrived early in the colonies and by the early 1600s was placed in South Carolina, and by the later 1600s had also found its way to Maryland.[7] Further, we must also note that Governor Spotswood himself was born in Morocco, and was likely familiar with Sephardic and Moorish émigrés from the Mediterranean to the New World. Spotswood's probable intent in traveling to the Blue Ridge Mountains was not merely to claim this territory for England—which had already been done—but rather to search for silver mines reputed to have been abandoned by the early Spanish colonists from Santa Elena. Thickening the matter further, is the fact that the Germania colony at which he stopped and took on men and supplies does not appear to have been settled by ethnic Germans, but rather Sephardic Jews from Holland and Bohemia who were specifically recruited by Spotswood for their mining and metallurgical expertise. (See the discussion and list of Germanna colonists in appendix 5.)

We should also bear in mind that the Spanish were still actively present in Florida, Louisiana, and other parts of the Southeast during this time period, and, further, that they and the English were hardly alone on the continent. In 1726, a man named Peter Sallings from Virginia was captured by Indians, traded to the Spanish, redeemed by the French and then sent to the Dutch. Withers, in his history entitled "Border Warfare," thus describes the captivity of Sallings:

---

[6]Lewis Preston Summers, *History of Southwestern Virginia 1746–1786 and Washington County 1777–1870* (Johnson City TN: Overmountain Press, 1903; repr. 1989) 38.

[7]Peden and Wright, vol. 6 of *Colonial Families of the Eastern Shore of Maryland*.

Sallings [Withers says] was taken to the country now known
as Tennessee, where he remained for some years. In company with
a party of Cherokees, he went on a hunting expedition to the salt
licks of Kentucky and was there captured by a band of Illinois
Indians, with whom the Cherokees were at war. He was taken to
Kaskaskia, and adopted into the family of a squaw whose son had
been killed. While with these Indians he several times accompanied
them down the Mississippi River below the mouth of the Arkansas
and once to the Gulf of Mexico.

The Spaniards in Louisiana, desiring an interpreter, purchased
him of his Indian mother, and some of them took him to Canada.
He was there redeemed by the French Governor of that province,
who sent him to the Dutch settlement in New York, whence he
made his way home to Virginia after an absence of six years.

In 1730, two men of probable Sephardic descent from Holland,
John and Isaac Van Meter, "obtained from Governor Gooch of Virginia,
a patent for forty thousand acres of land to be located in the lower
valley and this warrant was sold in 1731 to Joist Hite, of Pennsylvania,
who, in 1732, brought his family and sixteen other families and located
a few miles south of the present site of Winchester, VA. Emigration to
this new land was rapid and soon reached beyond the confines of Hite's
possessions.[8]

In 1750, Christopher Gist,[9] the son of Richard and Zipporah Murray
Gist of Maryland, was assigned to survey the lands surrounding the Ohio
and Mississippi Rivers. Gist was thirty or forty years of age and lived
with his family on the Yadkin River near the home of Daniel Boone on
the northern North Carolina frontier. The instructions given him by the
committee of the Ohio Company on 11 September 1750 were as follows.

You are to go out as soon as possible to the Westward side of
the great Mountains and carry with you such a number of men as

---

[8]Alexander Scott Withers, William Powers, and William Hacker, *Chronicles
of Border Warfare: or, A History of the Settlement by the Whites, of Northwestern Virginia: and of the Indian Wars and Massacres, in That Section of the State;
with Reflections, Anecdotes, &c.* (Clarksburg VA: J. Israel, 1831), as cited in
Lewis Preston Summers, *History of Southwest Virginia, 1746–1786: Washington
County, 1777–1870* (Richmond VA: J. L. Hill Print Co., 1903).

[9]Genealogical analysis suggests Christopher was of Sephardic Jewish descent.

you think necessary, in order to search out and discover the lands upon the river Ohio, & other adjoining branches of the Mississippi, down as low as the great falls, thereof; you are particularly to observe the ways & passes thro all the mountains you cross, & take an exact account of the soil, quality & product of the land, and the wideness and deepness of the rivers, & the several falls belonging to them, together with the courses & bearings of the rivers & mountains as near as you conveniently can; you are also to observe what nations of Indians inhabit there, their strength and numbers, who they trade with & what commodities they deal in.

When you find a large quantity of good level land, such as you think will suit the Company, you are to measure the breadth of it in three or four different places & take the courses of the rivers & mountains on which it binds in order to judge the quantity; you are to fix the beginning and bounds in such a manner that they may be easily found again by your description. . . .

. . . You are to draw as good a plan as you can of the country you pass thro; you are to take particular journal of all your proceedings and make a true report thereof to the company.

In compliance with the credentials received from the Ohio Company, Captain Gist, "accompanied only by a negro lad and a pack horse," set out from Wills Creek, the present site of Cumberland, Maryland, on his journey."[10]

Gist's travels led him through portions of eastern Kentucky, eastern Tennessee, and southwestern Virginia, and helped mark the trail for the Wilderness Road expedition of his neighbor Daniel Boone and the in-migration of the people who were to become known as Melungeons.

In 1754, 1755, and 1756, the French and Indians attacked colonial settlements in southwestern Virginia near New River, Reed Creek, and Holston River. A list of those killed, wounded, or taken prisoner has been preserved and is given below. It is instructive in that we see on it not only Scotch-Irish and English names, but also those whose names would seem to indicate Jewish/Moorish-Melungeon ancestry.

Adam Bingeman, New River, killed.
John Cook, New River, killed.
Henry Lin, New River, killed.
Nathaniel Welshire, New River, wounded.

---

[10]Summers, *History of Southwest Virginia, 1746–1786*, 47-48.

Dutch Jacob, New River, wounded.

His wife, New River, prisoner; escaped.

Frederick Stern, New River, wounded.

Mrs. Bingeman, Jr., New River, wounded.

Mrs. Davis, New River, wounded.

Isaac Freeland, his wife and five children, New River, prisoners.

Lieutenant Wright and two soldiers, Reed Creek, killed.

Colonel James Patton, New River, killed.

Caspar Barrier, New River, killed.

Mrs. Draper and one child, New River, killed.

James Cull, New River, wounded.

Mrs. English (Inglis) and her two children, New River, prisoners; scaped.

Mrs. Draper, Jr., New River, prisoner.

Henry Leonard, New River, prisoner.

Morris Griffith, Vause's Fort, prisoner; escaped

Robert Looney and a Dutchman, Reed Creek, killed.

John Lee, New River, killed.

Michael Motes, Reed Creek, killed.

Patrick Smith, Reed Creek, killed.

Moses Mann, Reed Creek, killed.

Valentine Harman and one son, New River, killed.

Andrew Moses, New River, killed.

Captain John Smith, Fort Vause, prisoner; escaped.

Peter Looney, Fort Vause, prisoner; escaped.

William Bratton, Fort Vause, prisoner; escaped.

Joseph Smith, Fort Vause, prisoner.

William Pepper, Fort Vause, prisoner.

Ivan Medley, and two daughters, Fort Vause, prisoners.

Stephen Lyon, Holston River, killed.

John Goodman, Holston River, killed.

Benjamin Harrison, Holston River, killed.

_____ Burk, Holston River, prisoner; escaped.

Mary Baker, Holston River, wounded.

Samuel Stalnaker, Holston River, prisoner; escaped.

Samuel Hydon, Holston River, prisoner.

Adam Stalnaker, Holston River, killed.

Mrs. Stalnaker, Holston River, killed.

Mathias Counie, Holston River, killed.

Michael Houck, Holston River, killed.

James McFarland, New River, killed.

John Bingeman, New River, killed.

Mrs. Bingeman, New River, killed.

Also settled in the area at the time were Peter Mathias, Adam, David, Jacob and Henry Harman, William and Richard Hall/Haile, Tobias, Philip and Joseph Clapp, Benjamin Angel, David Currie, Richard Hines, James Lyons, Richard Pearis (Peres), Nathaniel Gist (son of Christopher Gist), Joseph Martin, Elisha Walden, William Carr, William Crabtree, James Aldridge, Henry Scaggs, John Henry, Anthony Bledsoe, and John and Valentine Sevier (Xavier), all, I propose, of Sephardic/Moorish descent. By the 1770s, they had been joined by Robert and James Davis, Alexander Wylie, Hugh Gallion, John Berry, Andrew, Charles, and John Lewis, and a Lieutenant Goldman. And by 30 June 1777, nearby Moore's Fort had the following troops.

List of Troops at Moore's Fort—30 June 1777

James Alley; John Alley; Samuel Alley; John Barksdale; Andrew Cowan; Frederick Friley; Lewis Green, Jr.; Zachariah Green; Charles Kilgore; Robert Kilgore; John Kinkead; Alexander Montgomery, Sr.; Alexander Montgomery, Jr.; John Montgomery; Nehemiah Noe; James Ozburn (Osborne); Thomas Osborne; Patrick Porter, sergeant; Samuel Porter.[11]

On 22 July 1776, Virginia organized a battalion of soldiers from the southwestern portion of the state to battle the Cherokee Indians. Among these soldiers, as listed below, are several I propose to be of Separdic/Moorish descent.[12]

Adair, John*	Boggs, Captain Robert
Allison, Matthew*	Bradley, James
Anderson, Jacob*	Brausteter, Adam*
Arnold, James*	Brooks, Littleton*
Beets, James	Brown, William*
Bennett, William*	Buford, James
Berry, James*	Butler, Alexander
Berry, Thomas*	Caldwell, George*
Berry, George*	Campbell, James*
Bledsoe, Captain Isaac*	Campbell, Robert*

---

[11]Robert M. Addington, *History of Scott County, Virginia* (1932; repr.: Johnson City TN: Overmountain Press, 1992) 23-24.

[12]The reader is requested to compare the names on the following two lists with the lists of Sephardic surnames available at http://www.sephardim.com.

Campbell, Samuel*
Campbell, Captain John*
Carlock, Hanrist
Carney, Onsbey
Carson, David
Christian, Colonel William, 1st battalion
Cochran, John
Cocke, Charles
Cocke, Captain William
Coon, George*
Cougar, Jacob*
Crabtree, Abraham*
Craig, John
Crane, John
Crawford, William
Daugherty, James
Dougherty, Michael
Douglas, Samuel*
Drake, Benjamin*
Dunlap, Ephraim
Early, Jacob*
Eaton, Amos
Edmiston, William
Edwards, Nicholas
English, David*
Ewing, Samuel*
Fair, Samuel*
Farris, Gideon*
Finley, John
Finley, Robert
Fowler, Thomas
Frailey, Frederick
Francisco, Michael*
Frogg, William
Furnham, John
Gambell, Robert*
Gardner, Jacob*
Gay, Samuel*
Getgood, David
Gleaves, Michael
Goof, John
Gray, Captain Benjamin*
Greer, James*
Hamilton, James*
Hamilton, Francis*
Harris, James*

Harris, John Jr.*
Harris, John Sr.*
Hart, George, surgeon, 2nd battalion*
Haynes, William*
Helm, Leonard*
Henderson, Daniel
Henson, William
Henson, Jesse
Hicks, William
Higgins, Humphrey
Hobbs, Thomas
Hogart, William
Holston, Stephen
Hunter, David
Ingram, Samuel
Ingram, William
Irwin, Christopher
Irwin, David
Jennings, Jonathan
Jones, Cuthbert
Katherine, Francis
Kelley, James
Kendrick, Solomon*
Kid, Daniel
Lane, William*
Lane, Lambert*
Latham, John
Lewis, Colonel Charles, 2nd battalion*
Lewis, Captain Aaron*
Little, Valentine*
Little, Andrew*
Logwood, Thomas
Love, Philip*
McClanahan, Abraham
McClanahan, John
McCockle, James
McCormick, Joseph
McKenzie, David
McNutt, Robert
Madison, Captain Thomas
Markland, William
Martin, Jonathan*
Mason, James*
Meade, William*
Meads, Ebenezer*
Miller, George

Milum, William*
Mitchell, William
Montgomery, Captain John
Moore, Henley*
Morris, Gideon*
Muldrough, John
Mulhey, Jonathan
Murphy, Patrick
M'Cain, James
M'Carthy, James
M'Cormack, Daniel
M'Elheney, Robert
M'Farland, John
M'Farland, James
Nettles, William
Newland, George
Ocheltree, Michael
Ohair, John*
Onsbey, Arthur
Parker, George
Peoples, William
Phelps, John
Preston, Captain William
Preston, Robert
Ramsay, William
Ramsay, Thomas
Reburn, John*
Reins, Meredy*
Renfro, Joshua*
Rice, John*
Rice, William*
Rice, Charles*
Rice, Benjamin*
Richardson, James
Richardson, Henry
Riddle, Isaac*
Robinson, James*
Ross, William*
Ross, Edward*
Rounceval, Isaac*

Rounceval, David*
Rowland, Michael
Russell, Captain William*
Russell, Joseph*
Sawers, James*
Scott, Matthew
Sevier, Captain John*
Shelby, Major Evan, 1st battalion
Shultz, Christian*
Simpson, John
Smith, Thomas
Smith, David
Smith, Captain Daniel
Springer, Joab*
Starke, Joseph, surgeon, 1st battalion*
Stearns, Jacob*
Steele, James*
Stevenson, Robert
Stewart, Robert*
Talbert, Isbon*
Thomas, Richard
Thomas, Isaac
Thomas, Benjamin
Thompson, Captain James
Tuttle, James
Walker, John*
Wallace, David*
Wallace, Andrew*
Watson, Christopher
White, William
Whitner, Henry
Williams, Philip
Williams, James
Wills, William
Winters, Moses*
Womack, Jesse*
Wood, John*
Woodward, Lance
Young, James*

Nearby Washington County, Virginia listed the following settlers (1777–1784).[13]

Allison, Charles*
Anderson, Benjamin
Anderson, Jacob
Ayliott, James*
Barnett, Alexander*
Bates, Joseph
Bates, William
Baylor, John
Beattie, John
Beattie, William
Berry, James*
Berry, Thomas*
Berry, John*
Bowen, Charles
Bowen, William
Bowles, John
Bradley, John
Breckenridge, Alexander
Bryan, James*
Buchanan, George
Buchanan, Samuel
Caldwell, Thomas*
Campbell, Robert*
Carmack, Cornelius*
Carter, Thomas*
Clark, George
Cole, Hugh
Colvill, Andrew*
Cox, John*
Craig, David*
Craig, Robert
Cunningham, Jonath
Davis, Andrew*
Davis, John*
Doolan, James
Doran, James*
Dorton, William
Eaton, Amos*
Edmiston, John

Edmiston, Robert
Elliott, William
Evan, Andrew
Farris, Isaac*
Finley, George
Fowler, James
Fowler, John
Fulton, Thomas
Funkhouser, John*
Galbrath, Arthur
Gamble, Josiah*
Gamble, James*
Gilmore, William
Gray, Benjamin*
Greear, Andrew*
Griever, Philip*
Halbard, William
Halfacre, Michael
Hay, John*
Heard, Joseph
Helter, Abraham
Hobbs, Thomas
Holland, William*
Hope, Adam
Johnston, Curtis
Keewood, John
Keewood, Stephen
Kincannon, Andrew
Kinkead, John
Laughlin, Alexander
Lewis, Aaron*
Linder, Anthony
McElwee, James
McMillian, William
Mahon, David
Markland, William
Montgomery, William
Oglesby, Elisha
Outlaw, Alexander

[13]Summers, *History of Southwest Virginia, 1746–1786*, 267-69.

Piper, James*
Ramey, Daniel*
Rice, Henry*
Robinson, William*
Rosebrough, William*
Scott, William
Scott, Archibald
Sevier, John*
Sharp, John*
Smith, William
Smith, Thomas
Smith, John
Snoddy, John
Sproles, James
Steel, David*
Tate, William*

Tate, Thomas*
Teat, Robert
Tewell, Obadiah*
Topp, Roger
Vance, Alexander
Vanhook, Aaron*
Walker, William*
Wheeler, James
White, Solomon*
Whitney, Francis
Willoughby, Andrew
Womack, Jacob*
Wood, Jonathan*
Wylie, Alexander*
Young, Daniel*

From comparing these settler lists with lists of documented Sephardic surnames, it is apparent that several persons of Sephardic/Moorish ancestry are present at this time.[14] Contemporaneous with these settlers was Daniel Boone/Boon, America's archetypic pioneer. Boone had learned of Kentucky and the Cumberland Gap leading to it during the French and Indian War.

In June, 1769, Uriah Stone, Casper Mansker, John Rains, Abraham and Isaac Bledsoe, John Baker, and several others started from Reedy Creek of the New River and traveling down the Holston River passed, as did Boone and his companions, through Big Moccasin Gap, into Powell's Valley, and from thence on through Cumberland Gap into the territory of Kentucky. Furthermore, in the year 1770 the Long Hunters took the same route both in going to and returning from the valleys of the Cumberland and the Ohio rivers in which they hunted. In this way the most practical routes through the mountains into Kentucky were gradually becoming known at the time Boone first made his way to the border of the Bluegrass Region. Boone was so pleased with what he saw on his first trip that he returned to his family "with the determination," he says, "to

---

[14]Even John Sevier and his brother, Valentine, were of Moorish descent, the family (Xavier) having fled to France during the Inquisition. See Eloy Gallegos, *Santa Elena: Spanish Settlements on the Atlantic Seaboard from Florida to Virginia 1513 to 1607* (Knoxville TN: Villagra Press, 1998).

bring them as soon as possible to live in Kentucky, which I esteemed a second paradise, at the risk of my life and fortune."[15] Boone's party consisted of himself, his brother Squire, Benjamin Cutbirth, Michael Stoner, Richard Callaway, William Bush, David Gass, Edmund Jennings, John Kennedy, John Vardeman, James Nall, and others, about thirty in all. They cut and removed the underbrush and fallen timber from the "Trace" where the forest was dense, and blazed the trees along the Trace where the forest was open. They proceeded without encountering serious engineering difficulties, until they reached the neighborhood of Big Moccasin Gap. Among the earliest settlers in this newly opened area was Jacob Castle/Cassell who settled with his family at Castle's/Cassell's Wood (now Castlewood, Virginia). Concurrently, a James Greene arrived in 1772. He was followed shortly by a Captain John Blackmore, his brother Joseph Blackmore, son John Blackmore Jr., John Carter, and Andrew Davis, in 1773. Here they established Blackmore's Fort on the Clinch River. A certificate was issued for this in 1781 and witnessed by Jason Cabell, Harry Inness, and Nathan Cabell.

One of the other early families living at Fort Blackmore was Samuel Alley and his daughter, Polly, who was captured by Indians but later escaped. When reading through these historical events, I was suddenly struck by the names and returned to the listings of Sephardic and Moorish surnames and discovered that, with the exception of John Carter and Harry Inness, most of the other settlers appeared to be of Sephardic/Moorish descent.[16] Indeed, in his *History of Scott County, Virginia* (1932)

---

[15]Thomas Speed, *The Wilderness Road: A Description of the Routes of Travel by Which the Pioneers and Early Settlers First Came to Kentucky*, Filson Club Publications no. 2 (Louisville: J. P. Morton & Co., 1886; repr.: New York: B. Franklin, 1971).

[16]Volumes 1–9 of *Colonial Families of the Eastern Shore of Maryland* (Westminster MD: Family Line Publications, 1996–2000) were examined for Sephardic, Moorish, and/or Melungeon first names and surnames. Inspection of genealogies suggested that the following families were of Sephardic/Moorish descent. (Numbers in prantheses following family names are page numbers.) Vol. 1 (Barnes and Wright, 1996): Alley/Allee (2); Bellowes/Bellas (34); Davis (70-80); Hall/Hale (171); Hepburn/Habern (192-94); and Van Sandt (334-38). Vol. 2 (Barnes and Wright, 1996): Brisco (30-32); Nash (235-36); and Rasin (251-62). Vol. 3 (Barnes and Wright, 1999): Abrahams (7-8); Berry (35-47); Gibson (165-72); Lewis (252-55); and Parratt/Parrott (267-80). Vol. 4 (Christou

and Wright, 1998): Boon (37-39); and Davis (67-71). Vol. 5 (Peden and Wright, 2000): Denny (59-62); Jarman (102); Ratcliffe (177-82); Shepherd/Shepard (224-24); Sylvester (235-40): and Tate (264). Vol. 6 (Peden and Wright, 2000): Guilder/Gilder (67-68); Lewis (104-105); Van Bebber (18-188); Van Burkeloe (188-90); and Wood (204-206). Vol. 7 (Peden and Wright, 2000): Tilghman (231-41). Vol. 8 (Peden and Wright, 2000): Davis (72-82); Gale (123-28); and Holland (141-48). Vol. 9 (Peden and Wright, 2000): Collins (70-94); Quillen (227-29); and Rackliff (230-39).

See also *Early Families of Southern Maryland*, compiled by Elise Greenup Jourdan (Westminster MD: Family Line Publications, 1996). Vol. 5: Posey (33-46); and Moore (213-19). Vol. 8: Nash (108-109); and Briscoe (110-56).

Henry C. Peden, in *Marylanders to Carolina: Migration of Marylanders to North Carolina and South Carolina prior to 1800* (repr.: Westminster MD: Willow Bend Books, 2000; original 1994), provides descriptions of the backgrounds of the following persons from Maryland who "became" or intermarried with Melungeons: Alexander (2-8); Amos (9); Barber (15); Beall (17-18); Blackmore (21); Brazleton (24-25); Crabtree (38); Coward (38); David (41); Duckett (47); Fifer (54); Frizzell (57); Gaither (58-61); Gist (64-66); Griffith (60-70); Guyton (71-72); Haislip (72); Hale (72); Highat/Hyatt (80); Holland (82-84); Howard (85-88); Ijams (90-92); Jacobs (92); Jarman (93); Julian (95); Lewis (100); Lowe (103); Mace (105); Mosier/Moser (116); Nichols (119); Perry (125); Perryman (125); Ruth (180); Shepherd (141); Silver (143); Stoner (152); Vermillion (163); Wood (174); Beall (12); Berry (14); David (34); Dent (26); Eaton (42); Gallion (50); Gibbons/Gibbens (50); Horah (63); Lazenby (74); Lewis (75-76); Mace (80); Minor-Minner (91); Moser (92-94); Nichols (98); and Tate (125).

Western North Carolina Bible Records, collected by Lawrence E. Wood, Charles D. Biddix, and Wilma L. Muse (Asheville NC: Old Buncombe County Genealogical Society, 1992) lists the following families which I found to have predominately Sephardic/Moorish/Melungeon first names: Addington, Bryson, Burrell, Cabe, Clayton, Cunningham, Jacobs, Galloway, Holland, Kelly, Kerlee, McConnell, Moore, Moss, Penland, Russell, Saunders, Strain, Stanfield, Tatham, Van Hook, Williams, and Wilson.

The Washington County, Virginia, Historical Society in Abingdon has data bases for the following families I believe to be of Sephardic/Moorish/Melungeon ancestry due to their marriage and naming patterns: Alley, Aron, Austin, Bachman, Berry, Bingamins/Benjamin, Blakemore/Blackmoor, Boone/Boon, Chaffin, Elam, Cumbow, Galcia/Galevica, Gildersleeve, Gilley, Green/Greene, Hiatt/Hyatt, Jacobs, Judd, Latta, Lehero, Lewis, Morea, Oury, Paca, Parrigan/ Perrigan, Perry, Ramey/Remy, Rasnake, Ratliff/Ratcliff, Raya, Reeves/Rives,

Addington comments that the original spellings of Blackmore and Alley were Black-a-moor or Blackmoor and Allee or Ally. By 1776, a Samuel Cowan/Cohen had arrived with his family, and by 1794 they had been joined by James, John and Peter Van Beber, Vincent, Job and Abraham Hobbs, Adam Ely, and George Yokum (Joachim). By 1783, Daniel and Manasas Friel had opened a dry goods store in Abingdon, Virginia.[17] And by 1784 Joseph Gist, Samuel Weir, Ashael Rawlings, Andrew Greear, Valentine Sevier, and Archibald Stone had settled in Jonesborough, Tennessee. In essence, a small Sephardic/Moorish Melungeon community had formed in the midst of the Appalachian wilderness.

By the late 1700s and early 1800s these settlers had been joined by the North Carolina Melungeon families of Moses Shepherd, the Gillys, Henry Mershen, Ninian Steel, Joshua Furman, Austine Nicholas, Tyree Culbertson, and Freeman Beverly (a faith doctor). The Melungeon Dotsons, Pleasant and Nicholas Horne, the Rameys, the Benjamins, the Bollings, and the Bonds had also arrived. By 1815, John Berry, Cornelius Fugate, Jonas Wolfe, Isaac Low, and Goldman Davidson had joined the local militia. And in 1792 Nathan and Samuel Cowan/Cohen had opened stores in Knoxville and Jonesborough, Tennessee, while, in 1802, John Gold and Solomon Marks had become residents of Abingdon, Virginia. Further, by 1812 Daniel Sheffey, Benjamin Estill, Peter Mayo, Nicholas Van Stavern, Isaac Leftwich, and Baldwin Sisson were practicing law in Washington County. In other words, a virtual smorgasbord of Sephardic Jews, Moors, and Melungeons was now occupying a distinct section of Appalachia.

It is important, as well, to note that at least some of these early settlers may have originated from Spanish-held territories to the south. Spanish colonials of Moorish and Sephardic descent were still in danger

---

Sharrett, Sisson, Xavier, Yocum, Youel, Zion.

[17]Luther F. Addington, *The Story of Wise County, Virginia* (repr.: John City TN: Overmountain Press, 1988; Wise VA: Centennial Committee and School Board of Wise County, 1956) 117, notes that, during the 1700s and 1800s, the principal route to Wise, Virginia was through Abingdon, Virginia.

Paul Fink, in his *Jonesborough: The First Century of Tennessee's First Town, 1776–1876*, 2nd ed. (Johnson City TN: Overmountain Press, 1989) names Richmond and Baltimore as the primary trade routes to Abingdon, Virginia. From Abingdon, goods went to Wise, Virginia and on to Jonesborough.

of persecution by Spanish Catholic Colonial authorities. The fury of the Inquisition, which had forced them out of Spain in 1492, was still underway in the Americas. Crypto-Jewish and Crypto-Moslem settlers in New Mexico and Texas were still being burned at the stake through the 1700s.

The colonists in the Carolina colonies (who, I believe, were likely in large part of Sephardic and Moorish descent) were particularly hostile toward Spain. Led by Colonel James Moore, the Carolinians and their Creek Indian allies attacked Spanish Florida in 1702 and destroyed the town of St Augustine. Two years later, they destroyed the Spanish missions between Tallahassee and St. Augustine. The French continued to harass Spanish Florida's western border and captured Pensacola in 1719, twenty-one years after the town had been established.

Spain's adversaries moved even closer when England founded Georgia in 1733, its southernmost continental colony. Georgians attacked Florida in 1740, assaulting the Castillo de San Marcos at St. Augustine for almost a month. While the attack was not successful, it did point out the growing weakness of Spanish Florida. Britain gained control of Florida in 1763 in exchange for Havana, Cuba, which the British had captured from Spain during the Seven Years' War (1756–1763). Spain evacuated Florida after the exchange.

The British had ambitious plans for Florida. First, it was split into two parts: East Florida with its capital at St. Augustine, and West Florida with its seat at Pensacola. Britain attempted to attract settlers by offering land on which to settle and help for those who made products for export, but British rule lasted only twenty years. The two Floridas remained loyal to Great Britain throughout the War for American Independence (1776–1783). However, Spain—participating indirectly in the war as an ally of France—captured Pensacola from the British in 1781. In 1784 Spain regained control of the rest of the Florida as part of the peace treaty that ended the American Revolution.

Indeed, it was likely the retaking of Florida by the Spanish in the early 1780s that stimulated Sephardic Jews and Moors from the Carolinas and Georgia to migrate hurriedly to the greater safety of the Appalachians. Once there, kinsmen from Baltimore and Virginia arrived during the 1790s to enlarge the Melungeon communities. This Iberian-refugee migration continued through the early 1800s. In 1818, a twenty-three-year-old Jewish man from Baltimore, Jacob Howard, journeyed to Jonesborough, Tennessee and set up a print shop. He was financed largely by two local men of probable Sephardic ancestry, Elijah and Elihu Embree, who owned a local ironworks. In 1820, Howard began publishing *The Emancipator*, an antislavery newspaper with more than 1,800 subscribers nationwide. A later Howard publication, *The Farmers Journal*, was supported in part by Solomon D. Jacobs of Knoxville, Tennessee, who used it to advocate wider trade and transportation access for eastern Tennessee.

By the 1840s the area had attracted additional Sephardic and Moorish settlers: Isaac Stophel/Stofel and Zachariah Jourdan, Briscoe Baldwin, William Seymour, Jacob Newman and William Fleming, among others, were active in the political and commercial life of eastern Tennessee and southwestern Virginia. Contemporaneous members of preexisting Melungeon families included Elkanah Gilley, Adam Robinson, and James Gibson.

However, *none* of these individuals was apparently publicly labeled as *Jewish*. Where religious affiliations are listed for them, they are usually given as "Primitive Baptist." Many of these same persons are reported affiliated with the Freemasons lodges in Abingdon, Coeburn, and Wise, Virginia, and Jonesborough, Tennessee. In chapter 5, I will discuss in detail the significant correspondence between the Primitive Baptist faith and the Freemasons and outline why Sephardic Jews, Moors, and those who became known in Appalachia as Melungeons were affiliated with these groups. For our purposes now, however, it is appropriate that we simply acknowledge that none of those persons discussed so far was explicitly labeled in the documents I have seen as being Jewish or Moorish.

That other persons *were* seen as Jewish by these same historical writers is demonstrated in this excerpt from Paul Fink's *Jonesborough*:

> In 1853, two young German Jews, Herman Cone and Jacob Adler, brothers-in-law and in America only three or four years, came South looking for a place to locate. Reaching Jonesborough, they liked the place and the people, and the people, reciprocating, gave them a hospitable welcome. They opened a general store, and different from any of the other merchants, alternated weekly in keeping store and peddling in the surrounding country, in effect taking the store to the people. From the beginning, they were successful and took an active part in the life and affairs of the community. The store of Cone and Adler was in a two-story brick building on Main Street opposite the Chester Inn. Herman Cone lived in an adjoining frame house until he went back to Baltimore in 1870. Jacob Adler, in 1860, bought the brick

residence later known as February Hill, residing there until he too moved back to Baltimore in 1873.[18]

Here we see these two merchants (significantly from Baltimore, where so many of the earlier Sephardic settlers originated) clearly labeled and recognized as Jewish. Thus, as I will argue in chapter 5, among the Melungeons residing in Appalachia, their Judaic or Islamic traditions were either forgotten, submerged, or kept secret.

By 1856, several of the Melungeon inhabitants of Wise, Virginia had achieved political prominence. Among the justices of the peace were Melungeons William Roberson, Nicholas Horne, James Davis, Jeremiah Powers, Matthew Roberson, John Vanover, William Vanover, Charles Bond, and Jeremiah Bolling. The Rosenheim brothers had arrived to open a store on Main and Fifth Streets in nearby Bristol, Virginia. On 16 February 1856, Wise County, now heavily populated by "Melungeons" was formed from Russell, Scott, and Lee Counties. The names of the 121 persons who signed the act of incorporation for the new county were as follows.[19] (Several of these are my mother's ancestors, whom DNA testing has shown to have Iberian origins.)

Archer, William	Byrns, David
Baker, Jessee	Byrns, John W.
Baker, James	Carter, Granville C.
Beverly, William	Carter, Campbell
Beverly, Sylvester	Carter, C. W.
Beverly, Robert	Cooper, Hiram
Beverly, Robert Sr.	Cooper, John
Bickley, Hiram H.	Counts, Isaac
Bog, David	Dale, Hardin
Bogs, William	Dale, Hiram B.
Bond, William J.	Davis, John
Bruce, Daniel W.	Davis, William
Bruce, E. J.	Day, Due
Bruce, H.C.	Dean, Ellis
Buchanan, John	Dingus, O. F.
Buchanan, James Esq.	Eaton, Daniel H.
Buchannan, Morgan	Eaton, John

---

[18]Paul Fink, in his *Jonesborough: The First Century of Tennessee's First Town, 1776–1876*, 2nd ed. (Johnson City TN: Overmountain Press, 1989) 51.

[19]Charles A. Johnson, *A Narrative History of Wise County, Virginia* (1938; repr.: Johnson City TN: Overmountain Press, 1988).

Evans, Wilson
Freeman, Joseph
Gardner, Penecost
Gilley, John B.
Gilliam, John
Gilliam, William E.
Green, Hiram
Hall, Daniel
Hall, William
Hamilton, Robert T.
Hamilton, Schuyler
Hill, William
Hilton, Elisha
Hoge, Daniel S.
Horn, John P.
Horn, Jessee
Horn, Henry
Horn, Charles W.
Huff, James
Huff, Lorenzo
Huff, Charles
Hunsucker, George
Hunsucker, John
Hunsucker, James
Hunsucker, Jonathan
Ingle, Henderson
Ingle, James M.
Ison, Archebald
Ison, Isaac Jr.
Ison, Isaac Sr.
Jessee, Stanford L.
Jessee, David Jr.
Jones, James B.
Jones, Alfred T.
Jones, Benjamin
Kilgore, Ralph
Lane, Isaiah
Large, Charles
Lipps, Jacob
Lipps, Morgan T.
McCoy, Willie
McCoy, George W.
McFarlane, William

Musick, Z. N.
Osborne, Jonathan Sr.
Osborne, Eliza
Parsons, R. S.
Pilynor, George
Powers, Jonas
Powers, Jeremiah
Ramey, Daniel
Ramey, Daniel Jr.
Ramey, Jacob Jr.
Ramey, Jacob
Ramsey, James W.
Riner, Jacob
Riner, George W.
Robinette, Randolph
Shephard, Henderson
Skeen, A.J.
Skeen, Stephen S.
Skeen, Henry
Snodgrass, John H.
Stidham, Charles W.
Stidham, James
Stidham, David
Stidham, James D.
Stidham, Mart
Stidham, Jeremiah
Stidham, Adam
Taylor, James
Vance, David D.
Vance, Alexander
Vanderpool, Hezekiah
Vanderpool, James
Wampler, William
Wampler, George
Weaver, George
Wells, Anderson
Wells, Robert
Wells, Michael
Wells, Solomon
Wheatley, Parken
Wheeler, James C.
Willis, Absolem

Thus by the mid-1800s southwestern Virginia was populated predominately by persons I propose to be of Sephardic/Moorish ancestry, that is, Melungeons. Indeed, I believe the county itself was purposely established as a haven for persons of Iberian descent. The daughter of Governor Henry Wise of Virginia, for whom the county is named and by whom it was established, is listed as a Jewess in Stern's *First American Jewish Families*.[20]

The year 1856 also saw a tragic murder in Wise County. Alexander Carico, whose surname is unequivocally Sephardic but whose Judaic heritage had apparently been forgotten, was killed by his neighbor (also of Melungeon descent), Beverly Dickenson.

> Alexander Carico and Beverly Dickenson were neighbors, and lived in the neighborhood of Bull Run settlement. It is said both owned land and had settled there in the early pioneer days among the hills and wild woods of what is now the eastern part of Wise County, to dig out their living by the sweat of their brows. The country at that time was very sparsely settled and a large wild mountain range surrounded them.
>
> Time passed and one day, it is said, Alexander Carico found that some of his hogs had been shot and killed, and others crippled and the bells cut off some and shot off others. And some of his horses were found with their tails cut off. Carico accused his neighbor, Dickenson, of doing this and a grudge commenced between them and continued to grow.
>
> A footpath led through the low underbrush from the Primitive Baptist church that had been adopted as the courthouse of the county to the spring some two hundred yards in a southeast direction from the church. When the crowd heard loud talking and cursing and a dull low sound near the spring, people surged toward the spot. They found Alexander Carico stretched out upon the ground, unconscious. Beverly Dickenson, his neighbor had hit him on the back of the head with a large stick. The grudge had been rekindled and as they were leaving the spring, Dickenson in front with Carico close behind him. Dickenson remarked to Carico, it is said, "I have never cut off no cow bells or horses' tails," and Dickenson turned on Carico and struck him with a large stick.

---

[20]Malcolm H. Stern, *First American Jewish Families: 600 Genealogies, 1654–1988*, 3rd ed., updated and revised (Baltimore: Ottenheimer Publishers, 1991) 188.

Carico was at once carried to the home of Daniel Ramey, the monarch of the Big Glades, and first laid on a pile of rails in the yard of the Monarch's home. Dr. John Burns was called to Carico's side and at first pronounced him not seriously injured, but later Carico was carried and placed under the side of the Monarch's home and commenced to grow worse, and died sometime after midnight on 29th July, following.[21]

That Carico and Dickenson were both not following *kashruth* (Jewish dietary) principles is indicated by the fact that pork was part of their normal diet. Both also belonged to the Primitive Baptist church. But as we shall see in chapter 5, this particular faith was in many ways compatible with Sephardic Judaism.

Another tragic incident, this one in 1864 during the Civil War, suggests that at least some of those labeled as Melungeons had little in the way of formal education or religious instruction and were labeled as "persons-of-color." It is perhaps among these persons that the negative connotations of "Melungeon" in the larger community were grounded. It is also possible that these persons were descendants of the earliest and poorest Sephards/Moors dating from the mid-1500 Spanish settlements:

On the 5th day of February 1864, a young man by the name of Jacob Mullens, of Wise County, Virginia, was shot by order of Colonel Prentiss in West Abingdon at the location of the colored graveyard. Mullens had deserted from his company and joined the enemy. The Abingdon paper in speaking of Mullens says: "He was an exceedingly ignorant young man, almost a heathen, having never read the Bible, nor heard it read until after his conviction and never heard a sermon in his life. The chaplain of the post and several other ministers here gave him the benefit of their counsel and consolation, and he seemed to be penitent. He was greatly affected on the day of his execution, but exhibited a good deal of firmness and composure after arriving at the place of execution. He was sitting upon his coffin with his fingers in his ears when the order to fire was given. He expired almost immediately, five balls having pierced his breast.[22]

At the other end of the socioeconomic spectrum, Benjamin Gildersleeve served as a judge in the United States Circuit Court in Abingdon,

---

[21]Johnson, *A Narrative History of Wise County, Virginia,* 21-22.
[22]Summers, *History of Southwest Virginia, 1746–1786,* 532.

Virginia, from 1874 to 1884, as did Daniel Sheffey Lewis from 1882 to 1885, and George W. Levi in 1893.

Why Did Sephardic Jews and Moors Choose to Settle in Appalachia?

Perhaps the most nagging question arising from the foregoing analysis is *Why?* Why did large numbers of Sephardic Jews and Moors purposely migrate to Southern Appalachia, where at least some of them became labeled as Melungeons? The answer, I believe, resides in a serendipitous mixture of history and opportunity.

De Soto's 1540 Southeastern explorations, the twenty-year presence of the Santa Elena colony on the Carolina coast (1567–1587), the failed 1587 Roanoke Colony, and numerous Spanish and Portuguese shipwrecks, abandonments, and mutinies, both official and unofficial, off the Southeast's coastal waters created, by the mid- and late-1600s, a large mixed population of Jewish, Moorish, and Native American descent, which was fearful of the Spanish governments in Florida and Louisiana, but equally unlikely to ally themselves with England or France.

I believe these earliest "Melungeon" communities largely survived by hunting, farming, and trading on the outskirts of formal Spanish, English, and French colonies as these came and went. Dwelling in their own coherent communities, they owed allegiance to no nation and probably placed little trust in central governments or political authority.

During the early, mid-, and late-1600s and 1700s, their future numbers would be greatly supplemented by entire families of Sephardic Jews and Moors who immigrated first to the Netherlands, France, and Germany, and then to England, Wales, Scotland, and Ireland to escape the ever-widening violence of the Spanish Inquisition. After practicing their religions in secret (or openly in a few cases) in these waystations, many of these crypto-Jewish and crypto-Muslim families came to North American shores during the 1600s and 1700s. For example, one of my Melungeon ancestors, George Healle/Haile/Hale, arrived in the Virginia Colony in 1620 from Bristol, England. Other families of Sephardic Jews arrived from Welsh ports; others from Ireland and Scotland. Though labeled as "English," "Welsh," "Irish," and "Scottish," they were not ethnically or genetically Anglo-Saxon. Rather they were Sephardic Jewish and Berber. Similarly, as Kennedy has already pointed out,[23] many of the French Huguenots arriving in the South Carolina colony were actually Moors (or Sephardim); and were likely Muslim or Jewish rather than Protestant.

Upon arriving in North America, I believe, they quickly learned of the presence of others like themselves already settled in this new land and, over one or more generations, collected together in communities. (This will be discussed in chapter 6.) Within these communities, I further believe, they practiced their Judaic and Islamic religions, using Protestant-ism as a "cover."

I have already proposed that Wise County, Virginia was formed as a refuge for these crypto-Jews and crypto-Moslems in the mid-1800s. I now want to discuss this same idea of a Melungeon refuge or haven set a century earlier in what was to become eastern Tennessee. According to historians, for example, Dixon, Alderman, and Allison,[24] the first non-native transients in the Watauga area of Tennessee were Daniel Boone/Boon in 1760 and "transient traders" Andrew Greer/Greear (from whom I am descended) and Ceasar Dugger. The first permanent "white" settler (in actuality a Melungeon), William Bean, arrived in 1769 with his family and brothers-in-law George and John Russell from southern Virginia. Though labeled as "English" or "Scottish," these people were likely of Sephardic descent. In 1771, Jacob Brown/Browne, an "itinerant merchant from South Carolina"[25] from whom I also descend, settled on the Nolichucky River nearby. Brown(e) was a gunsmith and blacksmith, as well as a merchant, and opened a store on the river. On the nearby Holston River, John Carter (1737–1781), a merchant and land speculator

----

[23]N. Brent Kennedy with Robyn Vaughn Kennedy, *The Melungeons. The Resurrection of a Proud People. An Untold Story of Ethnic Cleansing in America,* 2nd rev. and corr. ed. (Macon GA: Mercer University Press, 1997) 126-27, 137.

[24]Max Dixon, *The Wataugans, Their History and Their Influence on Southern Appalachia and the Nation: American Revolution Roundtable* (repr. with index: Johnson City TN; Overmountain Press, 1989; ¹1976); Pat Alderman, *The Overmountain Men: Battle of King's Mountain, Cumberland Decade, State of Franklin, Southwest Territory* (Johnson City TN: Overmountain Press, 1986); John Allison, *Dropped Stitches in Tennessee History* (repr.: Johnson City TN: Overmountain Press, 1991; original: Nashville: Marshall & Bruce, 1897).

[25]Dixon, *The Wataugans,* 11.

from Amherst, Virginia arrived in 1771 and also set up a store to trade with the Indians and settlers. Like Brown, Carter was of Iberian descent (despite being labeled as "English") as recent DNA testing has shown. A photograph of his portrait and house are shown below.

John Carter portrait.

John Carter house.

On 17 March 1775, a consortium of these settlers and their financial backers purchased 20,000,000 acres of land from the Cherokees, including the entire Cumberland Valley and the southern half of the Kentucky Valley. Termed the Transylvania Purchase, this was the largest private land purchase in U.S. history. The purchase was negotiated with the Cherokees by Daniel Boone and included the following purchasers: Richard Henderson, Thomas Hart, Nathaniel Hart, David Hart, John Luttrell, John Williams, William Johnston, James Hogg, and Leonard Bulloch. An additional purchase was then made by Henderson of the land between Transylvania and the Holston settlements, which included the Cumberland Gap. This was subsequently sold to John Carter and his newly arrived partner, Robert Lucas.

Two days later, on 19 March 1775, the Watauga settlers purchased "all the land on the Watauga waters, land below the South Holston (river) and the Virginia line . . . the headwaters of the New River, consisting . . . of present-day North Carolina counties of Watauga, Ashe, and Alleghany.

In all [the purchases] amounted to 2,000 square miles, an area half the size of Rhode Island."[26] As Dixon further notes, it was called the *Watauga Country*. (Yes, *country*, not county.) Jacob Brown(e), my ancestral Jewish trader from South Carolina, then purchased several thousand acres, acquiring, as Dixon puts it, "a principality of his own."[27] The dwellers in Watauga Country, Carter's Valley, and Jacob Brown's Nolichucky Settlement then established a government that placed *no* requirements of religion, ethnicity, race, or social class on membership— the first such government in North America.[28] Dixon comments that the Wataugans "behaved as if they were independent" of all other governments. They not only constituted their own government, but also conscripted their own militia and "conducted negotiations with foreign powers": the British, the North Carolina colony, the Virginia colony, and the Cherokee Nation.[29] The chairman of the Watauga Association was John Carter and commissioners included Zachariah Isbell, John Sevier (Xavier), and Charles and James Robertson.

By the Eastern Seaboard British establishment, the Wataugans were viewed with fear and loathing and described, for example, as "Absconded debtors, indentured servants, and outlaws" (Indian agent Alexander Cameron, 1772), "Mongrels and barbarians" (British Colonel Patrick Ferguson, 1780), and "Fugitives from justice" and "off-scourings of the earth" (North Carolina legislator, 1784). But to me, of course, they were just gggg-grandfather and gggg-grandmother. So I guess one's opinion of the Watauga Country depends upon one's perspective.

The first formal religious institution in the Watauga settlement was Buffalo Ridge Baptist Church (1778), which, as will be described in chapter 6, was likely a crypto-Jewish meetinghouse. In 1778 and 1783, the Transylvania Purchase (though not the Watauga Association) was nullified by the governments of Virginia and North Carolina. However,

---

[26]Dixon, *The Wataugans*, 30.

[27]Dixon, *The Wataugans*, 31.

[28](1) James K. Huhta, "The Colonial Background of the History of Tennessee: A North Carolina Contribution," *The Tennessee Junior Historian* 1/1 (October 1968): 2-22. (2) *The Regulators in North Carolina: A Documentary History, 1759–1776*, comp. and ed. by William Stevens Powell, James K. Huhta, and Thomas J. Farnham (Raleigh NC: State Dept. of Archives and History, 1971).

[29]Dixon, *The Wataugans*, 21.

the investors were given 200,000 acres on the Green River in Kentucky and 200,000 acres in the Clinch River Valley and Powell River Valley in Virginia. Both of these territories were, and are, identified as primary Melungeon settlements.[30] In 1785, residents of the Virginia settlement, then termed Washington County, petitioned to prevent the teaching of religion in the public schools of the county. Petition signatories included John Berry, John Greene, Abraham Huyter, and H. Nunez—all of whom, I believe, were of Sephardic descent.[31]

---

[30]See, e.g., Kennedy, *The Melungeons.*
[31]*Appalachian Quarterly* 4/4 (December 1999): 32-33.

Chapter 5

Family Trees and Family Treks: Migration, Marriage, and Naming Patterns among the Melungeons

In this chapter, we will explore a key set of clues to Melungeon origins: their patterns of migration, marriage, and naming. Chapters 1, 3, and 4 documented the presence of Spanish settlements in the American Southeastern region during the 1500s and early 1600s. From this we learned that Sephardic Jews and Moors among the Spanish colonists would have been aware of travel routes, geological features, and Indian settlements in the area now encompassing Florida, Georgia, South Carolina, North Carolina, Virginia, and eastern Tennessee.

In chapters 3 and 4 it was proposed that the earliest inland settlers of these same regions, especially in Virginia, North Carolina, South Carolina, and Tennessee, were parties composed of Sephardic Jews and Moors who originated in Spain and Portugal. Some came to North America as Spanish colonists during the 1500s, while others fled to England, Holland, and France to escape the Inquisition during the 1492–1510 time period. After spending 100-150 years in these way stations, these Iberian refugees immigrated to the American shores along Maryland, Virginia, and South Carolina, and then, forming into family/kin groups, migrated with preexisting Iberian settlers to western North Carolina, western Virginia, western South Carolina, and eastern Tennessee. We now see that even the earliest Appalachian settlers such as Jacob Castle, Christopher Gist, John Blackamoor, and Samuel Ally were very likely of Jewish and/or Moorish extraction.

Let's take a detailed look now at four families. Two are famous, two are not famous, but have the virtue (?) of being my ancestors. It is instructive to examine lines of descent in terms of migration, marriage, and naming patterns. As we shall see, each of these leaves multiple signposts along the way, all saying "Melungeon."

The Boone Family

The ancestors of pioneer Daniel Boone are believed to have immigrated to England from France during the 1500s.[1] There was ample inflow to England during the sixteenth century of Sephardic Jews and Moors from several "way stations" in North Africa, Turkey, Italy, France, and Holland. Some of these Jewish and Muslim emigres chose to convert to Protestantism, while others retained their original faith. Those who remained Jewish or Muslim or converted to a "heretical" form of Protestanism (for example, Presbyterians, Quakers) were often encouraged to immigrate to the American colonies where they were promised a greater degree of religious tolerance, as well as free land, in return for serving as "English" colonists.[2] Such appears to be the case with the Boone family. Likely the name Boone was pronounced as *Bon* in France (perhaps it was *Bueno* in Spain). The earliest ancestor of which we have record is George (I) Boone (1597–1625), born in England. He possibly married either Ann Fallace and/or Joane Healle.[3]

George Boone's son, George II, married Sarah Uppey in England in 1665. They had four children: George III, Henry, John, and Percis (a daughter). Two of these children, Henry and John, were both baptized the same year, 1673, at the same church in England. They were likely between four and five years of age—quite late for a traditional baptism. Both remained, or were left, in England. George Boone III and his sister Percis (which, incidentally, is the Latinized form of the Greek *Persis*, "Persian woman") were *not* baptized and immigrated to Berks County,

---

[1] James Boone, "Our Genealogy" (1788?), appendix in Lyman Copeland Draper, *The Life of Daniel Boone*, as edited from the files and unfinished manuscript of Draper by Ted Franklin Belue (Mechanicsburg PA: Stackpole Press, 1998) 542-49.

[2] Esther Benbassa and Aron Rodrique, *Sephardi Jewry: A History of the Judeo-Spanish Community, 14th–20th* Centuries (Berkeley: University of California Press, 2002).

[3] The Healle family (from which I descend) emigrated to Virginia from England in the early 1600s. They married into several soon-to-become-Melungeon families—Perry, Chaffin—and migrated to Jonesborough, Tennessee in the late 1700s; there their name became Hale or Haile and they were listed as Melungeons.

Pennsylvania—a Quaker colony which received colonists of all faiths. To me, this pattern suggests that the Boone family split along religious lines during the 1670s, with a portion emigrating to the American colonies to practice Judaism while a portion remained in England as Anglicans. But, one may ask, how do we know they were Jewish and not, say, Quaker, since they settled in a Quaker colony?[4]

To answer this, let's look at the children of George Boone III who came to America. They were George Boone III who married a Deborah Howell; Sarah Boone who married Jacob Stover/Stuber; Squire Boone who married Sarah Morgan; Mary Boone who married John Webb; John Boone, who did not marry; Joseph Boone who married Catherine _____; Benjamin Boone who married first Ann Farmer and second Susanna Lycans; James Boone who married Mary Foukle and later Anne Griffith; and Samuel Boone who married Elizabeth Cassel (daughter of Arnold and Susannah Cassel). Now we are beginning to see French/Spanish and Hebrew given names and surnames entering the genealogy. Perhaps with religious freedom came greater naming freedom: no longer must we "act British."

By the next generation almost all pretense of "Britishness" vaporized from the Boone naming patterns. The son, Squire, who married Sarah Morgan (the daughter of Edward Morgan and Elizabeth Jarman (that is, German)) named their children Sarah, Israel, Samuel, Jonathan, Elizabeth, Daniel (the intrepid pioneer), Mary, George, Edward, Squire, and Hannah. Further, three of these children—Daniel, Mary, and George—all married into the Bryan family. This was a very common practice among Sephardic Jews and Moors, as it solidified kin networks and permitted religious practices to be conducted within the confines of a closely knit community.[5]

In the ancestry chart of the Boones prepared by James Boone, we discover first names such as Levi, Rebecca, Ina, Isaiah, Diadama, Deborah,

---

[4]Well, the most direct answer is because their descendants carry Sephardic DNA and practice Judaism! For example, actor Richard Boone, the seventh generation nephew of Daniel Boone, *is* Jewish.

[5]Stern comments that Sephardic Jews often married first cousins or uncles/nieces as late as 1858. Malcolm H. Stern, *First American Jewish Families: 600 Genealogies, 1654–1988*, 3rd ed., updated and revised (Baltimore MD: Ottenheimer Publishers, 1991) 173.

Daniel Boone (1734–1820)

Dinah, Jeremiah, Hezekiah, Abigail, Mordecai, Isaac, Josiah, Persis, Judah, Hannah, Anthony, Nathan, Ephraim, Rachel, Lurissa, Susanna, Samuel, Reuben, Michael, Noah, Jesse, Jonathan, Celia, Isabella, Joel, Jemima, Azor, Elijah, Isom, Enoch, Judson, Lavinia, Israel, and Medaria—a virtual smorgasbord of Hebrew and Mediterranean names.

Further, we see intermarriage with known Sephardic/Melungeon surnames: Cassell, Jarman, Carter, Van Cleve, Day, Brooks, Frank, Grimes, Tea, Pancoast, Davis, Klein, Mensch, Vastine, Questro, Simons, Coffey, Powers, Moore, Moss, Green, Ellis, and Hill. And we also see incremental generational layers of intermarriage among the Boones and Bryans—a pattern common not only to Sephardic and Moorish communities, but also among Melungeons.

But perhaps the Boones, for some unknown reason, are exceptional in their naming and intermarriage patterns. Evidence that they are hardly unique among those with Sephardic/Moorish/Melungeon heritage is provided by examining the genealogy of a second famous Melungeon family contemporaneous with the Boones and living in the same North Carolina/ Virginia/Tennessee/Kentucky area.

Abraham Lincoln

That Abraham Lincoln was of Melungeon descent was first suggested, to my knowledge, by Brent Kennedy.[6] Kennedy comments that Lincoln's mother, Nancy Hanks, was in all likelihood of Melungeon heritage, given several facts of her background. Indeed, anyone who looks at photographs of Abraham Lincoln is no doubt struck by his distinctively Semitic features: the thick, coarse black hair, the dark skin, dark eyes, prominent nose, and equally prominent cheekbones. So I was quite comfortable with Brent Kennedy's assertion regarding Lincoln's maternal ancestry. Then I came across a photograph of Lincoln's *paternal* cousin Mordecai Lincoln, in a history of Jonesborough, Tennessee book I had purchased.[7] There, in striking detail, were the same exotic, Melungeon features, but descended through the paternal, Lincoln, line. What if *both* Abraham Lincoln's parents had been of Sephardic heritage? This would certainly make sense, given what we have already learned of the endogamous marriage patterns for these people. To examine this hypothesis, I obtained a copy of journalist Ida Tarbell's book *Abraham Lincoln and His*

---

[6]See Brent Kennedy and Robyn Vaughan Kennedy, *The Melungeons. The Resurrection of a Proud People. An Untold Story of Ethnic Cleansing in America*, 2nd rev. and corr. ed. (Macon GA: Mercer University Press, 1997) 28-31.

[7]Paul Fink, in his *Jonesborough: The First Century of Tennessee's First Town, 1776–1876*, 2nd ed. (Johnson City TN: Overmountain Press, 1989).

Abraham Lincoln (1809–1865)

Ancestors.[8] Tarbell's treatise is written in the hyperbolic, worshipful language common to many biographies of the same period, yet it was especially useful to me for two reasons. First, Tarbell never doubted that

---

[8]Ida Minerva Tarbell, *Abraham Lincoln and His Ancestors*, Bison Books edition introduced by Kenneth J. Winkle (repr.: Lincoln: University of Nebraska Press, 1997), a reprint of the original, namely, *In the Footsteps of the Lincolns* (New York: Harper & Brothers, 1924).

her subject was of English extraction and a Christian. Thus she had no intention of promoting biographical details that might lead to the conclusion that Lincoln was, in fact, of Jewish descent. Second, she personally visited every site dwelled in by Lincoln's American ancestors, meticulously pouring through ancient deed records, wills, marriage certificates, and other artifacts detailing the lives of Lincoln's cousins, uncles, and neighbors. It is these myriad details that clearly suggest that Abraham Lincoln was, in fact, of Jewish descent.

According to Tarbell's account, Samuel Lincoln, aged seventeen or eighteen, from Hingham, England, journeyed as an indentured servant with Mr. Francis Lawes to Salem, Massachusetts in 1637. Several weeks after arriving there, young Samuel went to live with his older brothers Thomas and Daniel Lincoln and a cousin, Nicholas Jacobs, in New Hingham, Massachusetts (population fifty persons). These relatives had been in America for four years and had already established households. Also living in the community of New Hingham were Daniel Cushing, Israel Leavett, and the Rev. Robert Peck, a Puritan minister. Although New Hingham was officially a Puritan settlement, it is apparent that at least some of its fifty inhabitants were likely of Jewish origin (for example, especially Nicholas Jacobs and Israel Leavett).

In 1649, Samuel Lincoln married a local woman named Martha; their first child was a son named Samuel, born in 1650. In 1657, Martha gave birth to Mordecai, the child that was the ancestor of the president. Mordecai married Sarah Jones. In 1686, Sarah bore a son named Mordecai, and then in 1688 a second son named Abraham, after her own father.[9]

Mordecai Lincoln, Sr., was, according to Tarbell, a remarkably intelligent and industrious man. He built and operated a sawmill, a gristmill, and a forge, all functioning concurrently. He also mined and forged iron, one of the first American colonists to undertake this complex manufacturing process.[10] When Mordecai's first wife died, he remarried to a widow, Mary Chapin,[11] and had a third son, Isaac. (Mary Chapin herself had a

---

[9]Thus, it is likely that Sarah's family may have been Jewish, as well: Jones (Jonas) is a Sephardic surname.

[10]Notably, the Moors and Sephardic Jews of Iberia were especially skilled at ironworking. See Cecil Roth, The Spanish Inquisition (1937; repr.: New York: W. W. Norton, 1994, 1996) 46-48.

[11]According to materials available from the Jewish Genealogy Research Ser-

son named Jacob by her first marriage.) Hence our Hebrew naming pattern is continuing.

Mordecai and Martha Lincoln's two sons, Mordecai and Abraham, left home in their early twenties and went to Monmouth County, New Jersey. This colony freely accepted persons of any religious background as Tarbell duly notes.[12] Hence, this would have been an ideal spot for persons openly or clandestinely practicing Judaism. One of the prominent settlers in Monmouth was Richard Saltar, on whose land Abraham and Mordecai Lincoln established their own ironworks. Mordecai married Saltar's daughter, Hannah. Hannah's uncle was a Captain John Bowne (Boone), whose son's name was Obadiah.

Mordecai and Hannah Lincoln were prosperous in New Jersey. Hannah gave birth to a little girl, Deborah, who died only three years later and was buried in the Lincoln's private burial ground. When Hannah died, Mordecai moved with his five children to Berks County, Pennsylvania. Here he married Mary Robeson, whose surname is one of those most common among Melungeons.[13] Mordecai's children married into neighboring families in Berks County; significant among these were the Boones, including George Boone and his wife Deborah, and Squire Boone, the father of Daniel Boone. Mordecai's daughter, Sarah, married a Boone and Mordecai's son, Abraham, married another.

John Lincoln, Mordecai's eldest son married a widow, Rebecca Flowers Morris, in 1743, and settled in Lancaster County, Pennsylvania. Lancaster County was, like New Jersey, a multicultural area, having settlers from virtually all early American ethnic backgrounds and religions. Several of the Boones had also migrated onward to the area near Harrisonburg, Virginia in Rockingham County (then Augusta County). At the time, the population of the area was around 4,000 persons; several of them were to be later classified as "Melungeons."

John Lincoln died in Rockingham County in November 1788 and was buried in the family burial ground. He and his wife Rebeccah had three sons (Jacob, Abraham, and Isaac) and two daughters (Hannah and Lydia). In John's will he asks that God take his soul, but makes no reference to

---

vice (*Ikvot Avotaynu* "Footprints of our fathers," Chicago), Chapin was a variation of Chafin/Chaffin, the same Sephardic surname in my own lineage.

[12]Tarbell, *Abraham Lincoln and His Ancestors*, 31.

[13]See Kennedy, *The Melungeons* (²1997; ¹1994).

Jesus or salvation. John's oldest son, Abraham, married Bathsheba Herring in 1770. This Abraham Lincoln (grandfather of the president) took his wife, Bathsheba, and ventured to Kentucky with his friend and relative, Daniel Boone.

In 1782, at the outset of the great Melungeon migration to the Appalachians,[14] Abraham, Bathsheba, and their four children (Mordecai, Josiah, Mary, and Thomas) together with one of Bathsheba's brothers and Abraham's first cousin, Hananiah Lincoln, and their respective families set out for Kentucky. After arriving in Kentucky, Abraham began clearing land for settlement. In May 1785, while surveying land, he was killed by Indians.

Thomas Lincoln, upon the death of his mother, Bathsheba, in 1793, migrated to the Watauga Settlement in Tennessee, as previously discussed, a community of Melungeons. There Thomas lived near his uncle Isaac and Isaac's wife, Mary Ward (another Melungeon surname). Around four years later, however, Thomas returned to Kentucky to be near his brothers Mordecai and Josiah. Near their homes was that of Richard Berry (a Melungeon/Sephardic Jewish ancestor in my own lineage). On 12 June 1806 Thomas Lincoln married Nancy Hanks (also likely of Melungeon descent, as Kennedy discusses—see above) at the home of Richard Berry—this despite the fact that several churches were nearby.

In 1807, Thomas and Nancy Hanks Lincoln's first child was born, a daughter named Sarah; and on 12 February 1809, a son, Abraham, was born. Abraham, who was to become the sixteenth president of the United States, grew up on "Knob Creek Farm," Nelson County, Kentucky, where he attended schools taught by Zachariah Riney and Caleb Hazel. The Lincolns were members of Rolling Fork Church, originally affiliated with the Salem (Baptist) Association, one of several groups routinely called "Old Baptists" or "Primitive Baptists."[15] Thus there is strong genealogical support for the proposition that Abraham Lincoln was of Melungeon/Sephardic Jewish descent through both his paternal and maternal lineage. DNA analysis of Lincoln's remains could help confirm (or disconfirm) this proposal.

---

[14]And, as previously noted, the year the Spanish regained control of La Florida.

[15]The significance of this will be discussed in the next chapter.

Jefferson Davis—A Brief Excursion

Many early colonists surnamed Davis were of Jewish descent, including those in my own ancestry, so it seemed possible to me that the first (and only) president of the Confederacy might be Jewish as well. Information on Jefferson Davis's early ancestors is sketchy. They are said to have immigrated in the late 1600s or early 1700s from Wales, so many biographers quickly conclude he was Welsh. However, Wales, especially the town of Swansea, was a major port of embarkation for Sephardic Jews coming to North America during this time period.[16]

Jefferson Davis's great-grandfather, Evan Davis, was born in Philadelphia and, according to Allen, had migrated to a "Baptist community in South Carolina where he married the widow Mary Emory Williams and then crossed the upper Savannah River to settle in Georgia."[17] Their son, Samuel Emory—Jefferson Davis's father—was born there in 1756 or 1758. Samuel's mother had two sons by her earlier marriage, Daniel and Isaac Williams.

Samuel Davis and his wife Jane Cook moved to Todd County, Kentucky sometime around 1792 or 1793 after Daniel Boone's establishment of the first permanent (and Melungeon) settlements in that territory. Jefferson Davis was the tenth and last of the Davis's children, who included Joseph Emory, Benjamin, Samuel, Anna Eliza, Isaac Williams, Lucinda Farrar, Amanda, Matilda, and Mary Ellen. Allen describes Samuel Davis, Jefferson's father, as "unusually handsome with a mass of black hair, black eyes," and "an accomplished horseman." Jane Cook Davis, his wife, although "fair with large blue eyes," was a niece of Revolutionary War officer Major General Nathaniel Greene, of South Carolina.[18] Finally, Stern states that Elizabeth Johnson of Martinsville, Georgia, a niece of Jefferson Davis, was Jewish.[19]

---

[16]See Stern, *First American Jewish Families*.

[17]Felicity Allen, *Jefferson Davis: Unconquerable Heart*, Shades of Blue and Gray series (Columbia: University of Missouri Press, 1999) 32.

[18]Allen, *Jefferson Davis*, 34-35.

[19]Malcolm H. Stern, *First American Jewish Families: 600 Genealogies, 1654–1988*, 3rd ed., updated and revised (Baltimore: Ottenheimer Publishers, 1991) 96.

Jefferson Davis (1808–1889)

Although DNA analyses of Davis's descendants would be required to confirm his ethnic ancestry, the odds seem high that Davis was, indeed, of Jewish descent. If true, this would present the remarkable irony of two contemporaneous presidents of the United States—Davis and Lincoln—being Kentucky-bred Melungeons.

The Skeen/Evans/Sargeant Family

A third example comes from my own genealogy. The Skeen surname originated in Scotland. Peter Skeen was born in Pennsylvania in 1756 and came from all-Scottish forebears. This would at first glance seem to insure that his descendants would be primarily of Scottish-Protestant stock. However, this assumption neatly overlooks Peter Skeen's wife, Sarah Sargeant, whom he married in 1779 in Caswell County, North Carolina. Sarah came from two lineages that almost certainly were Jewish. First, her mother, Margaret Gold, was the daughter of Ephraim and Rebecca Gold. Second, her father Stephen Sargent had parentage from a Mary Green/Greene whose parents were Charles Green/Greene[20] and Elizabeth Iverson, daughter of Abraham Iverson. It is difficult to imagine that these ancestors were not Jewish, either of Sephardic or Ashkenazic origin. Thus, Sarah Sargent, wife of Peter Skeen, was either Jewish herself, or likely at least aware of her Jewish ancestry.

When Peter and Sarah married, they were living in Caswell County, North Carolina, and it was here that their first two children, William and John, were born. However, later sons Stephen and Jonathan and daughters Sarah and Nancy, and probably son Hiram, were all born in Laurens, South Carolina. It is possible the Skeens migrated to South Carolina because their Sephardic kin, the Greens and Sargents, were there.

In the second generation several children married partners of possible Melungeon ancestry, including Lydia Banyan, Susannah Kiser, and Meredith Evans. These family members had all migrated back from South Carolina to southwestern Virginia in the early 1800s, where they married and had children. This coincides with the acknowledged migration of Melungeons to the southwestern Virginia area from 1780 to 1820.

Further, Sephardic and Moorish names occur with greater and greater frequency within the Skeen genealogy once the relocation to Virginia and intermarriage with other possible Melungeons had taken place. Among these names are Ekza, Samuel, David, Daniel, Noah, Susannah, Nathaniel, Tabitha, Analin, Isaac, Alwilda, Allafair, Cannan, Elziah, Allie, and

---

[20]Green(e) is a common Jewish name now and was also common during the 1600s, 1700s, and 1800s among Jewish colonists. See Stern, *First American Jewish Families* (1991).

Sephronia. This was accompanied by an intense pattern of intermarriage with known Melungeon families, such as the Counts, Dotsons, Gilliams, Castos, Dobyns, Chafins, and Carricos.

Elizabeth Caldwell Hirschman

Lydia Jane Skeen Wampler, Emma Wampler Kennedy,
Marie Kennedy Carter, Virginia Carter Caldwell

In 1859, Lydia Jane Skeen married William Henry Wampler and they became my great-great-grandfather and grandmother. Photographs of Emma Wampler and her daughter, granddaughter and great-granddaughter (my mother), reveal a line of dark-skinned, dark-eyed women with straight, glossy black hair, high cheek bones, prominent noses, and strong chins. Most of these features are carried forward in me. However, the Skeens were not the only source for my Sephardic/Moorish features: due to endogamous marriage patterns, they also sprang from the high levels of Perrys, Davises, Chases, Hales, Berrys, Wolfes, Greens, Chaffins, and Brown(e)s in my immediate ancestry.

Dale Carter: An Unsung (Melungeon) Pioneer

After the Walter Perry Chase debacle (see chapter 4, above), I turned to the Carter family of Virginia for proof of my WASP heritage. Here, I thought, is the Real Thing, an English Englishman, Episcopalian, Virginia Tidewater plantation owner, elegance, good breeding, ties to the British aristocracy and even to William the Conqueror. I was ancestrally redeemed. I constructed an enormous ancestor chart that branched backward from the Virginia Carters through Lady Diana Skipwith and reached into several signers of the Magna Carta. I visited Norman castles in England, Scotland, Wales, and Ireland, secure in the knowledge that my ancestors Richard de Clare, Roger de Mortimer, and John de Lacy had built these, stone by stone and turret by turret. This is all still true.

However, since beginning my Melungeon quest I have now begun examining the distaff side of the Carter family—the wives—and found quite a different set of ethnic origins. This pattern began in 1695 when Captain Thomas Carter married Arabella Williamson on 22 August. The Williamsons also married into the prestigious Virginia Ball family. Miller notes that in both the Carter and Ball lineages four names taken from the Williamson family appear across several generations; these are Jesse, Jeduthan, Arabella and Margaret. Arabella is Spanish for "beautiful altar," Jesse ("God exists") is Hebrew and Jeduthan/Jeduthun is Arabic, meaning "the hand of the Prophet's companion."[21] I also learned that Williamson was a common Jewish surname in colonial Virginia.[22]

---

[21]Joseph L. Miller, *The Descendants of Capt. Thomas Carter of "Barford," Lancaster County, Virginia: With Genealogical Notes of Many of the Allied Families* (1912; current repr.: Harrisonburg VA: Carrier, 1997). Now available as "The Descendants of Captain Thomas Carter, 1652–1912" on "The Carter Family CD," from <http://www.rarebookreprints.com/Carterfamily.html>.

[22]See Stern, *First American Jewish Families* (1991).

Thomas and Arabella Williamson Carter had eight children. Their last child, Charles, my ancestor, moved inland from the Virginia coast to Amherst County, Virginia and married a woman whose name is unknown. (This may be a sign of possible Native American or Moorish ancestry, as the Carter family was quite literate and socially prominent.) Charles and his unknown spouse had eight children, five daughters— Judith, Lucy, Catharine, Susannah, and Elizabeth[23]—and three sons— John, Dale, and Charles. The three Carter sons all journeyed farther westward to the frontier.

On Thursday 6 October 1774 my ancestor Dale Carter, then thirty years old and the father of two, was killed and scalped by angry Shawnees outside Fort Blackmore. Seventeen miles away, at Moore's Fort in Castlewood, Virginia, Daniel Boone, the fort's commander, and a party of thirty men set out after the "marauding Indians," but failed to find them.[24] Dale's wife, Mary Bickley, was the daughter of John Bickley/ Beckley (for whom the town of Beckley, West Virginia is named). John Beckley served as guardian for Dale's children.

Dale's son John married Sarah Elizabeth Day[25] in 1791; their son Charles W. Carter married Hannah Berry (of Melungeon descent) around 1822; their son Granville Carter married Martha Cooper (of Melungeon descent) in 1853. Their son Mack Daniel Carter married Elvira Virginia *Chase* (who, we now know, was likely a *Perry*), a Melungeon. Their son, Daniel Edison Carter, my grandfather, married Marie Hagan *Kennedy*, a cousin to Brent's father, and the daughter of Lydia Jane *Skeen* Wampler, a Melungeon. The moral of this story is, don't ignore the wives!

Names as Social DNA

At the outset to this book, I listed surnames and given names typical of Melungeons. This chapter has traced in detail the carriage of given names across multiple generations for the Boones, Lincolns, Skeens, and Carters. I have done this because, after months of analysis, I believe that

---

[23]Notably, the names Judith, Lucy, and Susannah had not appeared in the Carter lineages prior to this.

[24]Miller, *The Descendants of Capt. Thomas Carter.*

[25]The surname Day is uncommon in English and likely was formerly *Dias*, "day" in Spanish.

names are used as a form of "social DNA," that is, they are carried across generations to signal one's membership in a specific family and a specific ethnic group.

It could be argued that, unlike genetic DNA, names can be "faked," "stolen," or "mistaken." And, yes, there is some evidence that the earliest Melungeon settlers likely Anglicized or replaced their original surnames as an attempt to fit in or escape the detection of their true origins (for example, my Perry-Chases). However, by the mid-1700s I came across little, if any, evidence of surname alterations designed to deceive or disguise one's ethnic origin. While phonetic spelling variations were common, surnames among the Melungeons remained relatively stable.

Much more significantly, Melungeon populations perpetuated a very distinctive set of *given names* which set them apart from the Scotch-Irish and English colonists and readily communicated their Judaic, Spanish heritage. In appendix 6 I have listed the most common given names among the early known Jewish American colonists. In it we see a virtual review of Melungeon given names for men and women. However, because Melungeons drew also from Arabic, Berber, and Turkish ancestors, their given names include some not found among contemporaneous colonial American Jews. Among these are Allafair, Mahalah, Pharabba, Mecca, Jemima, and Nimrod, Alley, Omar, Mosco (mosque), and Ishmael.

Further, there were some *Jewish* given names that occurred much more commonly among Melungeon populations than among colonial American Jews themselves. These include, for example, Elkanah, Resan, Mariah, Nannie, Vashti, Ina, Goldie, Rowena, Tabitha, Kezziah, Callie, Lula, and Rhoda (see appendix 2). Like genetic drift among physical DNA markers in a restricted population, over many generations the Melungeon's naming patterns drifted toward a unique set, and away from both the surrounding non-Melungeon and Jewish populations.

Chapter 6

The Templar/Freemason Connection

In the next two chapters we must solve two great mysteries. (1) First, how did Sephardic Jews and Moors from many points in Britain, Europe, and the Mediterranean, who had arrived in the Americas from the 1500s onward to the 1700s, gain knowledge of one another's existence and location? How did they then organize themselves and migrate en masse to the Appalachians? For this is just what the Melungeons did. By some remarkable process, from 1567 (or earlier) to the 1820s, they congregated, intermarried, and then migrated to distinct areas of Appalachia. What hidden force could have permitted such a large-scale, coordinated, mass movement of people to occur, all the while remaining undetected by the surrounding population? As we shall see, I propose that this phenomenal process occurred through the agency of *Freemasonry*.

(2) The second mystery to be solved is "where" did the Judaic and Islamic behaviors of the Melungeons "go"? If indeed, these people were—and are—of Sephardic and Moorish descent, why do we not now see synagogues and mosques when we drive through Appalachia? Where are the mikvahs, the rabbis, the Passover seders, the imams, the chadors that are part and parcel of the Jewish and Moorish heritage? The answer is, they are indeed there, but we do not recognize them, for they have been recast and relabeled. Our ancestors—the Melungeon Jews and Moors—have evolved into Baptists, but not just any Baptists; more specifically they have regenerated themselves as "(Old) Regular Baptists" or "Primitive Baptists," a Baptist subgroup with roots in the Appalachians and practices drawn directly from the Old Testament.

Freemasons: Who Are they?
And Why Should We Care about Them?

Before beginning research on the Melungeons I rarely thought about Freemasons. They were on the periphery of my consciousness, located in the same mental area as the Kiwanis Club, Rotarians, Knights of

Columbus, and the Hibernian Society—a sort of civic service community organization of middle-aged white men. . . . I was wrong.

Hasson Street, Rogersville, Tennessee

Masonic Temple, Rogersville, Tennessee

There is an old adage in science: correlation does not equal causation, which means that just because two events occur together, one does not necessarily cause the other. But sometimes it does. I had noticed, casually, that Freemasonry and Melungeons occurred together a lot. For example, the Wise County, Virginia grave of James A. Alley (b. 29 May 1890, d. 6 June 1935) and a descendant of the early Ally/Ali settlers at Blackamoor's fort has "a Masonic emblem, made of bronze, embedded in the stone."[1] Adams also reports that a "Dr. G. W. Dingus 1854–1929" has a Masonic emblem carved on both sides of his large monument in Wise County, Virginia.[2] (This grave is also set on an East-West axis, which is consistent with Jewish burial ritual.) Dr. Dingus was reputed to be of Melungeon descent. In this same graveyard are buried several other persons of probable Melungeon descent, including those having Davis, Bond, Carico, Ramey, and Castle surnames. And one of the graves even has a "grave house," commonly associated with Melungeon burial rituals.

But much more significant is the fact that virtually every town where the Melungeons settled also simultaneously had established a Freemason Lodge: this included Wise, Abingdon, and Coeburn, Virginia, and Jonesborough, Greeneville, Sneedville, and Rogersville, Tennessee. Indeed the correlation between Melungeons and Freemasons was becoming overwhelming, close to one hundred percent, which brings to mind another adage: Where there's smoke, there's fire.

At this point I stumbled across a "key" item that otherwise would have seemed innocuous: Pat Spurlock Elder, writing about how Sephardic Jews probably were *not* Melungeons, makes the simple statement that, "Fifteen Jewish families of Spanish-Portuguese origin arrived in Newport, Rhode Island in 1658 and introduced Freemasonry."[3] That did it! Freemasonry, I had learned by then, *was not publicly known to exist until 1717*, when an English lodge revealed itself. Here were Sephardic Jews arriving in America in 1658 already practicing Freemasonry. Now correlation had become, quite possibly, causation. I began reading every

---

[1]James Taylor Adams, comp., *Family Burying Grounds in Wise County, Virginia* (Wise VA: Wise County Historical Society, n.d. [1980s]) 120.

[2]Adams, *Family Burying Grounds in Wise County, Virginia,* 123.

[3]Pat Spurlock Elder, *Melungeons: Examining an Appalachian Legend* (Blountville TN: Continuity Press, 1999) 33.

book I could locate to find out what Freemasonry was and why Sephardic Jews and Melungeons were involved with it.

In his *Born in Blood: The Lost Secrets of Freemasonry*,[4] John J. Robinson reviews much of the prior literature on the Freemasons and proposes, as had other researchers before him, that the Knights Templar originated the secret society. Robinson notes that the Templar order, which was founded in Jerusalem in 1118 after the First Crusade, was headquartered on the site of the ancient temple of Solomon. Members of the order were called the Knights of the Temple, hence Templars. However, by around two hundred years later, in 1296, the Moslems had retaken the Holy Land and the Templars were pushed to the island of Cyprus. King Phillip V of France, financially indebted to the Templars, sought to "erase" his debt by simply destroying the order. On Friday 13 October 1307 all members of the order that Phillip could capture, were imprisoned, tortured, and killed.[5] Pope Clement V, an ally of Phillip's, did nothing to protect the Templars, despite the fact that its members had faithfully served the Holy Catholic Church.

Robinson argues that surviving members of the order, some of whom fled to Britain, while others fled to ports in the Mediterranean, developed a secret society, Freemasonry, which functioned to provide safe haven to fugitive Templars. As Robinson notes, much of the arcane symbolism employed by Freemasonry is derived from Solomonic myth and includes blood oaths and references to torture, murder, and charges of heresy, just as these were directed against the Templars. Robinson writes that Masonry is "a secret society of mutual protection. What the lodge was doing was assisting brothers in hiding from the wrath of the Church and State, providing them with money, vouching for them with the authorities, even providing the lodging that gave Freemasonry the unique term for its chapters and their meeting rooms."[6]

---

[4]John J. Robinson, *Born in Blood: The Lost Secrets of Freemasonry* (New York: M. Evans & Co., 1989).

[5]While both Friday and the number 13 have had evil connotations attached to them since very ancient times, some regard this event in 1307 as the origin of the modern superstition that terrible events may occur on Friday the 13th.

[6]Robinson, *Born in Blood*, xviii. Indeed, since the Masons originated in France, the term "Mason" likely is an English corruption of the French *maison*, which means house or dwelling. As Robinson, and others, have commented, the

I agree with Robinson's analysis, but believe it is incomplete, for there was another group living in close proximity with the Templars which was concurrently being harassed by the Roman Catholic Church—the Sephardic Jews. As Robinson himself notes, only a year before Phillip murdered the French Templars, they had seized the assets of the French Jews:

> As a covert operation, the concept of simultaneous apprehension was not totally new. In a similar plan the year before [Philip] had effected the arrest and imprisonment of every Jew in France on one day, 22 July 1306. A few weeks later, in accordance with the master plans, the Jews were all exiled from France, but without their property. Their cash was taken directly into Philip's treasury and arrangements were made for auctions of their chattels. Then it was announced that the crown of France had also taken possession of their accounts receivable, and the state became a very efficient collection agency, demanding that all sums due to the Jews of France be paid to the lawful holder of those accounts, the exchequer of France. Correspondingly, of course, all debts owed to the Jews by the state were cancelled, just as Philip expected that in a suppression of the Templars all debts owed by the state to the Templars would also be cancelled. The simultaneous arrest of every Templar would take a similar operation, but one made more complex because the group to be arrested contained many experienced fighting men.[7]

Thus, the Templars and Jews both found themselves "on the run" from France and the Catholic Church early in the 1300s. For this reason, it is not likely coincidental that the first-known Freemason texts, termed the "Old Charges," appeared the same year that the Jews were experiencing violence from the Church, that is, in 1306.

According to Robinson,[8] Freemasonry "charges" or regulations in these old documents included "That no member is to reveal any secret of any brother that might cost him his life and property." Another charge was that no visiting brother was to go into a town without a local brother to "witness" for him. A known local witness could provide a believable

---

Mason iconography of trowel, angle, and other construction/building images came much later, during the 1800s.

[7]Robinson, *Born in Blood*, 130.

[8]Robinson, *Born in Blood*.

cover story and verification of a real or assumed identity. Most important, the resident brother could steer the visitor away from the people and places that might cause questions to come up.

Still another charge was that the visiting brother be given employment for two weeks, then given some money and put on the road to the next lodge. Robinson continues:

> On the run, the fugitive would have one overriding concern, which was to not be caught. That meant traveling off the main tracks, preferably with a guide or with directions provided by a friend. In a village or smaller town he would be most vulnerable, because a stranger would be easily spotted. His next major concerns were something to eat and a safe place to sleep, with the latter far more stressful to him. Eating can be done at odd times on the move and even postponed for long periods. Sleeping cannot be put off beyond the point at which the human body absolutely demands it, and then the fugitive is at gravest risk. . . . Safe lodging would have been an imperative. . . .
>
> At the next stop, he would need a device or signal by which he could locate the man who was to befriend him there and by which he could safely identify himself. Later in that same century, Lollards hiding from the church would use the line, "Let's drink from the same cup," as a means of establishing their identities. The Freemasons developed a much more elaborate system by which a Mason had a sign by which to identify himself (his "due-guard"), a sign to appeal for help to any brother who might be present (the Grand Hailing Sign of Distress), words to use in darkness or to direct to others who might be out of sight or looking in another direction ("O, Lord my God, is there no help for a Son of the Widow?"), and even a confirmatory catechism ("Are you a traveling man?" "Yes, I am." "Where are you traveling?" "From west to east.").[9]

It is this network of Freemasonry which I believe helped guide the outgoing groups of Sephardic Jews and Moors displaced by the Spanish and Portuguese Inquisitions of 1492 and 1497 to their safe havens in France, Holland, Germany, North Africa, Italy, and Turkey, and subsequently guided them over a 200-year period—from 1567 to 1790— to America and ultimately to Appalachia.

---

[9]Robinson, *Born in Blood*, 162-63.

Jewish Symbolism in Freemasonry

Some Freemasonry Symbols

When I am not out tracking down my Melungeon ancestry, I am a professor and consultant in advertising imagery and cultural symbolism. Thus, when I encountered books on the Freemasons, especially that of

Beresniak and Hamani, *Symbols of Freemasonry*,[10] I found it quite remarkable that Masonic imagery was so obviously grounded in Jewish symbolism, especially that of the Kabbalah—the branch of Judaism that deals with, among other things, the mystical meanings of Hebrew numbers and Hebrew letters. Significantly, Kabbalism was developed by Sephardic Jews; thus it made sense that these same persons who were persecuted in France, Spain, and other Mediterranean countries would utilize their own secret symbols to establish codes known only to themselves and a few trusted others. The Templars, of course, having dwelled for centuries among the Jews (and Moslems) of the Levant would similarly be knowledgeable of this same set of codes.

Outside the Alamo

Let's take a closer look now at these symbols. First, Beresniak notes that "the Masons of the Ancient and Accepted Scottish Rite[11] use the

---

[10]Daniel Beresniak, *Symbols of Freemasonry*, photographs by Laziz Hamani (New York: Assculine Publishers, 2000).

[11]Scottish rite Masonry originated in France and established the earliest system of Masonic iconography. As we shall see, this system of symbols was used subsequently in the Appalachians to establish and maintain smuggling operations.

Hebrew months and a calendar based on Jewish chronology, or *anno hebraico*. . . . This calendar begins in mid-September and adds 3,760 years onto the Gregorian calendar. . . . At the grade of the Royal Arch, the date of creation is 530 B.C., the date when building was started on the second [Jewish] temple by Zerubabel. . . . At the degree of Royal and Select Master . . . time begins with the dedication of Solomon's temple, that is to say, in 1,000 B.C."[12]

Beresniak continues by quoting from the Masonic *Thistle* manuscript of 1756: "Nimrod [son of Cush and grandson of Ham, the youngest son of Noah, and a powerful king—Gen. 10:8-12] created the Masons and gave them their signs and terms so that they could distinguish themselves from other people."[13] Thus, the Masons, like the Jews and the Templars, are a people set apart.

In addition, Masonic lore echoes Judaic theology by ascribing great meaning to the east-west axis. Significantly, Islamic and Jewish (and Melungeon) funerary rites require the body to lie on an east-west axis with feet pointed toward the east, toward Jerusalem (from which the Jews, Moslems, and Templars all sprang.[14] Masonic lodges are also aligned on an east-west axis with the entrance to the west and the Grand Master seated on King Solomon's throne, to the east. To Masons, the east signals knowledge and enlightenment, just as Jerusalem does to Jews and Muslims.

Further, Masonic meetings begin with the lighting of candles, as does the Hebrew Sabbath celebration. Two pillars are set at the entrance to the Masonic lodge, labeled Jachin and Boaz. Here there is a direct intake of meaning from the Kabbalah:

---

[12]Beresniak, *Symbols of Freemasonry*, 18.

[13]Beresniak, *Symbols of Freemasonry*, 26. "Nimrod," a fabled ancient Mesopotamian/Assyrian hero-king figured largely in ancient Hebrew literature. Perhaps *not* so coincidentally, several Melungeon lineages include Nimrod as a given name.

[14]Addington states that among the early (Melungeon) settlers of the region, "The family burying place was usually a sunny knoll *facing the east*. Most of the time a very brief burial service was conducted at the grave. More elaborate funeral services were preached later on, generally a year from the time of interment." Luther F. Addington, *The Story of Wise County, Virginia* (repr.: John City TN: Overmountain Press, 1988; Wise VA: Centennial Committee and School Board of Wise County, 1956) 52.

The pillars are described in three biblical passages: 1 Kings 7, 15-21 and 2 Chronicles 3, 15-17 and 4, 11-13. All three descriptions, although markedly different, name the right-hand pillar Jachin and the left-hand one Boaz. In the Masonic rites, Jachin is translated as "may it establish" or "may it affirm" and Boaz as "with strength." The Hebrew word for pillar is *amoud* (plural *amoudim*), from the root letters *ayin, mem,* and *daleth* which means "to stand, to be upright, to be situated there." As for the symbolism of the letters to which the cabbalists attached a great importance because they give life to the meaning of the words (a cabbalistic adage says "let the letters in the words come alive"), it goes as follows: *ayin* is the eye, *mem* is the origin, water, and mother, and *daleth* is the door.[15]

Masons carry a double-edged sword, which also has a meaning originating in the Old Testament:

The straight-bladed sword has two cutting edges and a handle in the shape of a cross. All the members of a lodge have such a sword, which they use during ceremonies. The curve-edged sword is known as "the flaming sword" due to its shape. This is an allusion to Genesis 3, 23-24: He banished the man and in front of the garden of Eden he posted the great winged creatures and the fiery flashing sword to guard the way to the tree of life. The flaming sword is held by the Worshipful Master (the president of the lodge) during initiations to the grade of Apprentice and is laid on his tracing board while the lodge works.[16]

Other relevant symbols are the *acacia,* an evergreen which grows in the desert and is discussed in the Bible; the *olive tree,* whose oil was used by the Jewish revolutionaries, the Maccabees, to light their lamps for Hanukkah; the *Ark of the Covenant,* which carries the ten commandments God gave to Moses; the *Seal of Solomon/Star of David* symbol which is outlined by the Masonic emblem of the compass and square.

Finally, the sons of Freemasons are termed Lewises (sing. Lewis) and are granted automatic entry to the order at age twenty-one, as a birthright. This parallels the Hebrew tribal name of Levi (Lewi), which is passed automatically from father to son. The Levites/Levis were a priestly class among the ancient Hebrews.

---

[15]Beresniak, *Symbols of Freemasonry,* 44.
[16]Beresniak, *Symbols of Freemasonry,* 29.

The Meaning of It All

Beresniak's summary statement of the purpose of Freemasonry is "to gather what is scattered."[17] And what was scattered at its inception during the fourteenth and fifteenth centuries were the Templars (as Robinson rightly observes) and also the Sephardic Jews and Moors—all collective victims of the Roman Catholic Church. That Sephardic Jews were early among the Masonic membership is indicated by Robinson's notation that an Elias Aschmol (Ashmole) was a British Freemason in 1646, and further that the colony of South Carolina, founded by Anthony Ashley Cooper, the Earl of Shaftsbury, was organized along Masonic principles by Cooper, who was a Mason. As Robinson notes, "South Carolina became a bastion of Freemasonry in the United States, which it still is. The city of Charleston was the port of entry for what became Scottish Rite Masonry, when it was introduced from France."[18] Further, Stern affirms that Sephardic Jews were leaders in the Savannah, GA Masonic lodge. From 1735 to the 1760s, Sephardic Jews streamed into Savannah; two of them, Moses and Daniel Nunez, were leading figures in the Savannah Masonic Lodge.[19]

And, of course, as we are now aware, South Carolina and especially the area around Charleston, were the entry points for a large influx of Sephardic Jews and Moors—from 1567 at Santa Elena to 1743 with the Purrysburgh colony and beyond.[20] The people who were to become Melungeons either were Masons or had friends and family members who were. I propose that Masonry served as the communication mechanism through which "those which are scattered" could be brought in an organized fashion to many safe harbors in the New World.

In the Company of Pirates and Corsairs. Charles Hudson, writing about the Juan Pardo Expeditions (ca. 1567) on behalf of the Smithsonian Institution, noted that Spanish artifacts recovered from Santa Elena were identical to items recovered in Rhea County and Greene County,

---

[17]Beresniak, *Symbols of Freemasonry*, 8.

[18]Robinson, *Born in Blood*, 285.

[19]Stern, *First American Jewish Families*, 3rd ed., 164.

[20]A list of the Purrysburgh settlers is provided in appendix 3. Although purportedly a "Swiss-German Protestant" colony, Purrysburgh was, very likely, composed of Moors and/or Sephardic Jews from Southern France.

Tennessee: both were areas where early Melungeons settled. The men on Juan Pardo's expeditions, especially a Sergeant Moyano, believed rich deposits of silver and valuable crystals were to be found in the Appalachian Mountains and set off on several excursions to locate these riches. Mines of corundum crystals, potentially quite valuable according to Hudson, were located and recorded in the Pardo expedition's notes.

Apparently the Spanish did begin mining operations in the Appalachians near Hendersonville, North Carolina. Hudson states that:

> Perhaps the most substantial of these reports is a discovery made by geologist Deane F. Kent (personal communication). In 1942 he found a complex sulphide vein (copper, lead, zinc, pyrite, etc.) in a granite gneiss. At the site he found the inscription, "JAN MDLXVII" (1567) chiseled into the rock. He also found a small pig of lead with a Spanish coat of arms and a six-sided gun barrel about 18 inches long. The site is east of present-day Hendersonville, North Carolina, about 36 miles from Joara, so that four days or less would have been required for a round-trip prospecting excursion.[21]

Hudson continues by noting that

> one of the best-documented instances of European artifacts comes from a mica mine in Macon County, North Carolina. When the Guyer mine was opened up in 1875, a shaft was found that was cleared to a considerable depth. Between depths of 35 and 50 feet, several iron implements were found. These include a socketed axe of an "old pattern which is now [i.e., in 1881] rarely met with." It was a light axe, with the blade and head each about 3¾ inches in width, narrowing between them into 2¾ inches. A maker's mark appeared on the blade, but it was too worn to be read.
>
> A second tool was a wedge measuring 3¾ inches long by 1½ inches wide. And a third tool appears to be the two prongs of a pickaxe that was broken at the socket. Frederick W. Simonds, who reported this discovery, erroneously interpreted the two pieces of the pickaxe as a pair of "gudgeons," i.e., parts of a windlass [sic]. It is possible that it

[21]Charles M. Hudson, with documents relating to the Pardo expeditions transcribed, translated, and annotated by Paul E. Hoffman, *The Juan Pardo Expeditions: Explorations of the Carolinas and Tennessee, 1566–1568* (Washington DC: Smithsonian Institution Press, 1990) 167.

was a pickaxe of such an ancient form that it was completely unfamiliar to him.

If the Spaniards did any mining in the area that Pardo explored, they must have done it between 1602 and 1700. Two pieces of historical information, both based on hearsay, argue for this. One is Francis Yeardley's account of men in his employ who in 1654 went by boat to Roanoke Island and then to a Tuscarora hunting quarter in the interior. Yeardley says that the Tuscaroras told them about a Spaniard who had been living in their main town for seven years. He was said to be very rich, with thirty people in his "family," including seven negroes. . . .

The other incident occurred in 1690, when James Moore traveled from the Carolina coast to the mountains searching for ores and minerals. He later reported that he had found seven different sorts of minerals and ores, which he later sent to England to be tested. At one point in his travels he said that he was told by some Indians that some Spaniards had been at work in mines just 20 miles away. The Indians described to him "bellows and furnaces," and said that they had killed these Spaniards, because they were afraid that they would enslave them and put them to work in the mines.[22]

I have made this detour into archaeology to illustrate that the "Spanish," in this case very likely Sephardic Jews and Moors who had come not merely to settle the New World but also to escape the Inquisition back home, were engaged in clandestine operations at the far edges of Spanish colonization in the 1600s. It is also likely that Governor Spotswood of Virginia, born in Morocco where he could have become acquainted with Sephardic Jews and Moors,[23] had learned of possible treasures in the Appalachian mountains, and made his 1716 trip, accompanied by more Sephardic Jews and Moors, to the Blue Ridge in search of these treasures.

In his book on the Freemasons, Robinson makes much of the fact that a central pledge in Masonry is that the initiate must "join the brotherhood of pirates and corsairs."[24] Robinson argues that the Templars were an important element in the Barbary pirates/corsairs of the 1500s and 1600s,

---

[22]Hudson and Hoffman, *The Juan Pardo Expeditions*, 192.

[23]In *Melungeons: Examining an Appalachian Legend* (Blountville TN: Continuity Press, 1999) 122, Pat Spurlock Elder states that Spotswood was born in Morocco.

[24]Robinson, *Born in Blood*.

a group which Kennedy has already noted were heavily drawn from exiled Moors and Jews.[25] The corsairs owed allegiance to no flag or state and engaged in all manner of illegal activity from smuggling to slave trading. Because we have no "official" references whatsoever to Spanish-authorized mining activities in the Appalachians during the 1600s and 1700s, it is fair to assume that those being conducted by the "Spanish" were occurring on a surreptitious basis. Gold and silver obtained not only from mining activities, but also precious metal plundered through piracy and theft could have been what was being smelted in the "bellows and furnaces" reported by the Indians to James Moore in 1690.

Significantly, one of the most long-lived legends in the Appalachians—Swift's Silver Mine—concerns just such a clandestine operation. The September 1997 issue of *Appalachian Quarterly* devotes five articles to a discussion of "Swift's Silver Mine." As a young child visiting my grandparents in Norton, Virginia, my grandfather (who I now know to be of Melungeon descent) used to tell me that somewhere in the surrounding mountains was a fabulous silver trove worth "millions of dollars," whose exact location was unknown. According to my grandfather, D. E. Carter, the silver was not ore, per se, but rather silver bars or coins that had been hidden. They were contraband (illegal) and the man who had hidden them had died before retrieving them. My grandfather, a skilled hunter and woodsman, had searched for the hidden horde, but had not been able to locate it, although he did take me to see a small cave, now empty, that had been "used by people a long time ago."

Since there has never been any geological evidence of silver *ore* in this area of the Appalachians, I have to agree with several of the *Appalachian Quarterly* article authors, as well as Brent Kennedy, that the silver was likely smuggled/stolen refined silver, which was being converted to counterfeit currency. And further, that the clandestine operation was being conducted by Melungeons with the possible assistance of Freemasons in Richmond, Charleston, and Savannah, all of which were major shipping ports during this period. The persons allegedly involved in the original "mining" operation, James Ireland, Samuel Blackburn, Isaac Campbell, Abram Flint, Harman Staley, Shadrach Jefferson, and Jonathan Munday, lived in North Carolina near the Yadkin and Catawba Rivers during the 1750s—an area and time period when Sephardic Jews and Moors had

---

[25]Kennedy, *The Melungeons*, 2nd ed., 113.

migrated from Baltimore to this area of North Carolina. And according to available genealogies, all of the men had Sephardic/Moorish ethnic connections. According to the legend, they began their search for "mines" in 1760. The following year they were joined by Joshua McClintock, Henry Hazlitt, Seth Montgomery, Moses Fletcher, John Motts, Alexander Bartol, and Jeremiah Bates, of the same ethnic heritage.

Also connected to the story in various ways is Robert Alley (that is, Ally/Ali) a relation of the Ally's of Fort Blackmoor, Jacob Castle/Cassell, Valentine Lorentz and various Freemasons including Levi Todd, Samuel January and Robert Patterson. Further, the "mine" itself was supposedly inscribed with a compass marked "N,S,E,W," a central Masonic emblem.[26]

While I don't want to belabor this point too long, I do want to make clear that accepting a connection between Freemasonry and Melungeon/ Sephardic/Moorish colonists in Appalachia goes a long way toward tying together archaeological, genealogical, historical, and folkloric knowledges, which previously were disconnected. What once were fractured bits of information can now be connected into a coherent explanation.

A Final Word on the Masons

On a recent trip to Tennessee (to attend the Melungeon Gathering at Vardy, June 2001), I acquired an 1883 book titled *Tennessee Templars* by James Daniel Richardson.[27] Published in Nashville, it presents brief

---

[26]Michael S. Steely's book on Swift's silver mine also mentions that the group of men transporting the silver were collaborating with the "Scottish Company" to ship the treasure "across the seas," which I interpret as a reference to Scottish Rite Freemason pirates. Additional Freemason iconography cited by Steely includes the trowel and square symbol and the sheepskin apron worn by Masons during their ceremonies. As if these were not enough clues, he also notes that the counterfeited coins were both French and Spanish (who were both still actively trading in the Mississippi area through the 1700s), and that the silver "mining" group was also working with the "Mecca" Indians (i.e., the earliest Islamic Melungeons) who lived in the area. See Steely's *Swift's Silver Mines and Related Appalachian Treasures* (Johnson City TN: Overmountain Press, 1995).

[27]James Daniel Richardson, *Tennessee Templars. A Register of Names, with Biographical Sketches, of the Knights Templar of Tennessee, and Brief Histories*

biographical sketches of the Knights Templar of Tennessee, who were Scottish Rite Freemasons. Lest anyone still be in doubt as to the Masons' ability to communicate with one another internationally, and "gather what was scattered," I list below the persons who were members *in Tennessee* having immigrated from overseas. The reader is also invited to hypothesize as to their ethnicity.[28]

Name	Origin
George Stodart Blackie	Aberdeen, Scotland 1834
Emmanuel Bolli	Pernambuca, Brazil 1841
George Cade	London, England 1829
Frank Cahill	Thurles, Ireland 1832
Vincenzo Castello	Pavia, Italy 1851
George Cowan	Balley Kelley, Ireland 1842
Eugene Falconnet	Berne, Switzerland 1830
William Frederick Fisher	Mecklenburg, Germany 1846
Harry Forsdick	Suffolk, England 1850
Aaron Gerdland	Sweden 1838
Carl Casper Giers	Bonn, Prussia 1828
Rodolf Hafeli	Paris, France 1850
Lionel Hawkins	Oxfordshire, England ____
Adolphus Heiman	Potsdam, Prussia ____
George Hoff	Steinweiler, Germany 1838
Thomas Marsh Horsfall	Everton, England 1838
David Daniel Jons	Liverpool, England 1847
Joseph Kinney	Yarmuth, Nova Scotia 1827
Frank Lamont	Waterford, Ireland 1845
William Richards	Dublin, Ireland 1842
John Henry Rolffs	Freiburg, Germany 1842
William Rowen	Limerick, Ireland 1831
Charles Scherer	Germany 1840
George Sieferle	Baden 1813
Edward B.Stahlman	Leusso, Germany 1843
William Stewart	Fifeshire, Scotland 1808
Albert Benjamin Tavel	Neuchatel, Switzerland 1843
August Wilde	Setten, Germany 1851

---

of the Grand and Subordinate Commanderies, "Prepared under orders of the Grand Commandery" (Nashville: R. H. Howell, 1883).

[28]I compiled this list from Richardson's discussion in his *Tennessee Templars*.

Chapter 7

Keeping the Faith:
How Jews and Muslims Gathered Together
and Became Baptists

At the outset of the previous chapter, I promised to discuss not only the relationship between Freemasonry and Melungeons, but also to describe how the Jewish and Muslim heritage of these people became transformed into being "Baptist." I was raised as a Presbyterian and did not have any Baptist friends, so I knew very little about their religious beliefs and practices. In fact, the only thing I did know was that Baptists required full-immersion baptism, rather than the "water sprinkled on the baby's head" ritual we Presbyterians engaged in.

In this case, my ignorance turned out to be very beneficial, because rather than relying on my own store of possibly fallacious knowledge, I instead purchased two excellent ethnographies on Southern Appalachian Baptist denominations by Howard Dorgan, an Appalachian State University professor of Religion and an expert on Southeastern religious practices. Dorgan is not a "Melungeon researcher," is not seeking out Sephardic Jews or Moors, and is not expecting to see Freemasons lurking in the background. He just writes about what he observed over a decade's worth of fieldwork at several Baptist fellowships located in eastern Tennessee, southwestern Virginia, eastern Kentucky, and western North Carolina. He also includes several photographs of the Baptist churches and their members engaged in a variety of worship activities.[1]

I became interested in the possible linkage between some Baptist sects and Melungeons when, as with the Freemasons, I kept seeing a

---

[1]Howard Dorgan, *Giving Glory to God in Appalachia: Worship Practices of Six Baptist Subdenominations* (Knoxville: University of Tennessee Press, 1987; repr. 1989, 1990).

repetitive correspondence between these two entities. Wherever the Melungeons were, there would be specific kinds of Baptists: "Old Regular Baptists" or "Primitive Baptists." The correlation between early Melungeon identity and membership in a "Primitive" Baptist church or association was close to one hundred percent. I knew there had to be a connection. I also was searching for the religious outlet for the Melungeons' traditional Judaic and Islamic beliefs. I felt very strongly that these faiths could not simply have evaporated. Yet there were no recorded synagogues or mosques in early, or late, Appalachian settlements. Where had the Boones, Blackamoors, Allys, Cassells, Angels, and all the others practiced their faith?

Ironically, Patricia Spurlock Elder, a researcher hostile to much current Melungeon theorization, provides us with the answer. Historically, Elder suggests

> Melungeons were Baptist, especially "Primitive Baptist." The first Separate Baptist Church in Virginia was located on the Dan River—the heart of early Melungeon country. Harris says Louisa County was mainly Baptist with congregations coming from three sources: early immigrants who settled the southeastern part of the state, settlers from Maryland circa 1743, and settlers from New England.[2]

Now this is interesting, indeed, as traditional history informs us that the English and Scotch-Irish settlers of this period (who were *supposed* to be living in Virginia) were Presbyterian, Episcopalian, and Methodist. However, in fact we have independent Baptists flowing in from New England (for example, the Lincolns), Maryland (for example, the Hailes, Perrys, and Chafins) and from southeastern Virginia (for example, the Skeens, Carters, Boones, and Blackmoors). Further, the first churches established in Kentucky were also not Presbyterian, Episcopalian, or Methodist, but once again, Primitive Baptist.[3]

An informative example of this is provided by commentary in the December 1999 *Appalachian Quarterly* regarding the Austin family:

---

[2]Pat Spurlock Elder, *Melungeons: Examining an Appalachian Legend* (Blountville TN: Continuity Press, 1999) 108-109.

[3]Malcolm Hart Harris. *History of Louisa County, Virginia*, new ed. (Richmond VA: Dietz Press, 1963; 1st ed., 1936) 189. In 1748, the Camp Creek meeting and others have Samuel Bunch, his family, and several Moorman families on their rosters.

Jesse and Margaret Austin were born in North Carolina, died in Wise County, Virginia and were buried in the Austin Cemetery in the south of the mountain near Pound, VA. The family moved to a farm on Toe River in Ashe County, NC, in 1855, then to Russell County, VA (now Wise County) in 1857. In 1858 they moved to the head of Elkhorn Creek (now Jenkins) in Letcher County, KY. . . . Jesse Austin was a farmer and an excellent surveyor, but was best and farthest known as a minister of the Primitive Baptist faith. Children: Matilda Ann, Seralda N., Andrew Jackson, Anne Reeves, Margaret Jane, Jesse Franklin, David Washington, William Douglas, Julia, Mahala E., Thomas Jefferson, and Jerusha Austin.[4]

In the photograph accompanying the story, Jesse is shown with a full, untrimmed beard and Margaret's entire head is wrapped in a black veil, termed a *chador*, a Sephardic and Muslim traditional apparel head covering for women. Note also that their children bear both Jewish and Islamic names, that is, Mahala and Jerusha.

In the June 1999 *Appalachian Quarterly* we are given a discussion of some Baptist churches in Kentucky:

According to Spencer,[5] it appears that the first families in the Boonesboro (KY) settlement were all Baptists; it is known that the Boones, Calloways, and Frenches were Baptist. According to Collins History, the first marriage was performed there 7 August 1776 between Samuel Henderson and _____ Calloway by Squire Boone, a younger brother of Daniel, who was a Baptist preacher.[6]

And the June 1997 *Appalachian Quarterly* carried an article on the Goins-Minor Melungeon family that describes in detail their adherence to the Primitive Baptist Church:

Zephaniah Goins, son of John Going and Elizabeth Going, and my seventh-generation grandfather, was born about 1758 in Halifax County,

[4]*Appalachian Quarterly* 4/4 (December 1999): 13.

[5]Information is taken from John H. Spencer, revised and corrected by Burilla B. Spencer, *A History of Kentucky Baptists from 1769 to 1885*, vol. 1 of 2 (repr.: Lafayette TN and Dayton OH: Church History Research & Archives, 1976 and 1984; original 1885).

[6]Sandi Goren, "The Old Baptist Churches," *Appalachian Quarterly* 4/2 (June 1999): 71-73.

Virginia. He enlisted in the Virginia troops during the American Revolution and was present at the Battle of Yorktown when Cornwallis surrendered in October 1781. Zephaniah Goins, a Melungeon, was married to Elizabeth Thompson 20 June 1790 by Rev. Joseph Anthony of Henry County, Virginia. She was the daughter of William Thompson and Mary Estes Thompson.

Learning that Zephaniah Goins and Elizabeth Thompson Goins had joined Blackwater Primitive Baptist Church by dismission letter from another church which was unnamed, I began trying to locate this church. . . . While searching in the public library in Kingsport, Tennessee, I found the minutes of neighboring Stoney Creek Primitive Baptist Church at Fort Blackmore, Virginia, just across the state line. They contained some very interesting Melungeon references in the minutes recorded in 1813. The term "Melungeon" was probably in common usage long before then, but this is the first time I have found it recorded. Fort Blackmore was built at Stoney Creek, in Washington County, Virginia before the Revolutionary War by Capt. John Blackmore to protect the settlers from Indian attacks. Fort Blackmore was located about eight miles southwest of present day Dungannon, Virginia in Scott County.

. . . .

Grandfather Thomas Bledsoe was in Capt. Blackmore's command. He filed his Revolutionary War pension application in Hawkins County 24 April 1834. He was born in March 1760 in North Carolina and moved with his parents to the new territory, about 7 miles from Long Island of the Holston River, on Reedy Creek. It is now the site of present day Kingsport, Tennessee.

The Ft. Blackmore Stoney Creek Primitive Baptist Church minutes are complete from 1801 to 1811. The first minutes dated 14 November 1801 reveal that it was an existing church and adding new members rapidly. Meetings were held on the *second Saturday* of each month. The minutes reveal that the congregation was composed of whites, Melungeons, free Negroes and slaves. During the next four years, eighty-eight new members were added; thirty-three of these were persons bearing familiar Melungeon names: Gibson, Collins, More [Moore], Bolin, Bolling, Sexton, Osborne, Maner and Minor, while others bore surnames suggesting Jewish or Muslim ancestry: Abbel, Bama, Cornelius, Alley, Israel Davis, Broobachs, Estep, Rhea.[7]

---

[7]*Applachian Quarterly* (June 1997): 90-92.

After years of study, ethnographer Howard Dorgan writes cryptically of the Old Regular and Primitive Baptist faiths, "I cannot explain why this variation of the Baptist denomination developed in Central Appalachia."[8]

Both faiths are based upon a very minimalist set of strictures. Notably these Baptists view themselves as the chosen people, they take the Bible, both Old and New Testaments, literally; they believe in full-body adult baptism; they engage in other bathing (foot washing) rituals, and do not send their ministers to a central training facility, but rather permit them to emerge from the congregation. What is absent from this doctrine is any mention of Protestant or Catholic theology, such as the Nicene Creed and the Apostles Creed, which developed subsequent to the Old and New Testaments, and with which denominations such as Presbyterianism, Methodism, Lutheranism, and Congregationalism are heavily laden.

However, in conjunction with this stripped-down, biblically based doctrine come several unique practices. First, women and men are segregated within the Primitive and Old Regular Baptist Churches. Only men may become preachers and take an active role in church administration. Women sit in separate, posterior areas of the sanctuary and in some congregations even enter through separate doors. Both these practices are common to Sephardic Judaism and Islam, but not Protestantism or Catholicism. Women are further instructed to wear unrevealing clothing, apparel that covers their bodies fully and is not in any way enticing to male eyes.[9] Sephardic Judaism and Islam do likewise. Further, women are instructed not to cut their hair, also Jewish and Islamic practices not found in Protestantism or Catholicism.

During the sacrament of the Lord's Supper, actual wine (not Protestant grape juice) is served and actual matzoh (described by Dorgan as a "hard, flat pancake bread") is served to members; both the wine and matzoh are prepared at home by members. This is consistent with the

---

[8]Dorgan, *Giving Glory to God in Appalachia: Worship Practices of Six Baptist Subdenominations*, 243.

[9]A photograph of Susannah Bond Lawson in Melungeon apparel, that is, an all-black dress with head covering, long sleeves, and floor-length skirt, appears on p. 810 of *Coeburn, Virginia, Area History: Celebrating the Centennial of the Town of Coeburn* (Coeburn VA: compiled and published by the Coeburn Kiwanis Club, 1994).

Jewish celebration of Passover, but inconsistent with common Protestant and Catholic practice.

Religious services often begin on a Saturday, when a business meeting is held, and are carried over to Sunday. In earlier days, Saturday services were the norm (see the description of the Blackmoor Fort Baptist Congregation). Further, days were counted from sundown the evening before, instead of from sunrise. Both these practices are consistent with Judaism rather than Christianity.

Many Primitive and Old Regular Baptist churches carry Old Testament names. Among those listed by Dorgan are Zion Hill, Mount Carmel, Mount Zion, Mount Ephraim, Mount Ararat, Samaria, Lebanon, Bethel,

Rebecca, Elizabeth, Little Sarah, Little Martha, Naomi, Little Ruth, Little Rachel and Canaan's Hope. Dorgan includes many photographs of the exteriors of the churches. These show them to be plain, simple, unadorned, and functional in appearance. There is no steeple, no cross, no bell tower, no stained glass window, no arched ceiling. The churches are usually placed in unmarked, out-of-the-way locations, in places where only knowledgeable congregants could find them, and had few windows.

The interiors of the churches are bare of religious art, crosses, and other forms of iconography, except sometimes for photographs of the (male) past preachers along the back wall. Musical instruments are not used; singing is done by a process known as "lining" wherein a song leader will call out the lines of the song and the congregation will sing them back.

The churches generally operate in an autonomous fashion, belonging only to loosely constructed "correspondences" with other, usually close-by, congregations.

Thus, Primitive and Old Regular Baptist practice bears a strong resemblance to some traditional Jewish worship rituals. The lack of religious iconography, the portraits of patriarchs (rabbis), the chanting of the cantor, and the absence of instrumental accompaniment echo Judaic practice. The secretive locations and absence of external signage are ideal for churches who do not want to be "discovered" by unwanted guests.

Baptisms were/are conducted in lakes or rivers where enough water was present to completely immerse the individual. Only adults were/are baptized, as children and infants were/are deemed too young to make such a religious commitment. In one photograph Dorgan shows congregants praying after a riverside baptism; several of the men are crouched head down, just as Muslims at prayer. Indeed, the entire concept of ritual bathing is much more consistent with Islamic cleansing and Judaic mikvah (ritual bathing) practices, than it is with Protestant or Catholic tradition.

Further, Carol Huff in an *Appalachian Quarterly* article on Old Regular Baptists states that at baptisms "men dress in white shirts and dress pants, the women in long white dresses. Both men and women cover their heads with white cloths. . . . Afterwards there is much rejoicing in the neighborhood. . . . The family of the new church member will have a huge dinner to celebrate."[10]

Also, as with some Sephardic Jews and Muslims, Primitive Baptists and Old Regular Baptists have communal meals on their cemetery grounds once a year. Usually a tree-canopied shelter or brush arbor (very similar to those used in the Jewish harvest-festival observance, Sukkot or Booths) will be used for a memorial service naming the deceased and recalling their lives. In particular, male elders are eulogized and their contributions recited. The women prepare an elaborate meal, which is served at the outdoor site. At this time, graves are frequently groomed (for example, swept with a broom) and decorated with flowers. This

---

[10]Carol Huff, "The Old Regular Baptists," *Appalachian Quarterly* 5/4 (December 1999): 84-86.

service combines elements of Jewish and Islamic religious practice, with the large exception that *pork* is always available in various forms, especially country ham. (My sense here is that the consumption of pork lost its taboo status shortly after the Melungeons arrived in the New World. Domestic and feral pigs were a much more readily available meat source than cattle or sheep, especially in the Appalachian Mountains.)

We close this chapter with Dorgan's description of the Primitive and Old Regular Baptist communal foot-washing service. Here we see interspersed elements of the Jewish Passover, with its wine and unleavened bread, the Jewish mikvah, or ritual bathing, and, remarkably, a ceremonial flourish seemingly adopted from Freemasonry.

> It may come as a bit of a shock to realize that many of these Southern Appalachian Baptist fellowships use actual wine in their enactments of the Last Supper. I had always supposed that the traditional Baptist attitude toward alcoholic beverages would preclude the use of real wine. But in this Baptist service a somewhat cloudy home-fermented substance was poured from three large Log Cabin syrup bottles into several common cups. The bread also was homemade, a heavy, unleavened loaf broken into thumbnail-size bits for serving. Deacons of the church handled this serving with an unrushed solemnity, taking the bread and wine to the people as they sat in their pews.
>
> After all participants had been served and the materials of the communion had been cleared, the fellowship moved directly to the foot washing part of the service. Several metal basins, pitchers of water, and white towels were brought to a table in front of the pulpit. The procedure was a simple one. If you wished to wash a fellow worshiper's feet, you moved to the front of the church, took one of the towels and tied it ceremoniously around your waist, poured water into a basin from one of the pitchers, and moved out into the congregation where that brother or sister was sitting. You knelt before that individual, removed her or his shoes, and then dipped each foot separately into the basin, while cupping your free hand into the water and gently pouring water over the top of the foot. As each foot was finished, you then took the free end of the towel and dried that foot.[11]

---

[11]Howard Dorgan, *Giving Glory to God in Appalachia: Worship Practices of Six Baptist Subdenominations* (Knoxville: University of Tennessee Press, 1987; repr. 1989, 1990) 120-21.

What I especially want to draw attention to in this passage is the seemingly innocuous statement that any person desiring to wash feet took a white towel and "tied it ceremoniously around your [his/her] waist."[12] When I tried to mentally envision this, it did not make practical sense. Why tie the towel around your waist, if you are going to use it to dry? Why not simply drape the towel over your arm? I was reviewing my materials on Freemasonry for the prior chapter and rereading Robinson's *Born in Blood* when two passages leapt out at me. The first was that several British Masonic Lodges claimed John the Baptist (upon which the Baptist denomination is based) as one of their patron saints. Thus, to these Freemasons, following John the Baptist's admonitions as to full immersion to cleanse oneself of sin would be requisite practice. The second passage that caught my attention, however, was even more stunning. Robinson, discussing the Freemason initiation ceremony, writes: "Then occurs an especially intriguing part of the ceremony, the presentation of the Masonic 'apron.' This is now frequently of *white cloth or felt*, but the old usage would require that the apron be of *white lambskin . . .* , simply a whole lambskin *tied about the waist*."[13] Thus, this Freemason symbol may have entered the Baptist ritual as well.

Melungeon religious practices appear to be an amalgam of the Old Testament and the New; of Judaism, Islam, and Christianity; a mélange of all that has guided this people spiritually and kept them safe in their mountains: matzoth at communion, pork with Passover, Jesus Christ praised by rabbinical preachers, chanted gospel melodies, baptisms in the mikvah, loose-fitting dresses and chadors. Their synagogues and mosques are to be found in the mountains; they are up narrow, winding roads, unmarked and isolated from the stranger's gaze. Their names could read Zion and John the Baptist, Moses and Calvary, Exodus and Easter—intertwined to eternity.

---

[12]In her *Appalachian Quarterly* article on Old Regular Baptists (see n. 9 above), Carol Huff even terms this "girding" with the towel.

[13]John J. Robinson, *Born in Blood: The Lost Secrets of Freemasony* (New York: M. Evans & Co., 1989) 207.

Chapter 8

We Are Not Alone:
"Melungeons" around the World

The Spanish and Portuguese Inquisitions displaced a million persons between the years 1492 and 1506—200,000 Sephardic Jews and 700,000 Muslims.[1] While many of the Sephardis fled eastward to Turkey, Greece, and Italy, and many of the Moors crossed back over the Straits of Gibraltar to North Africa, others from both groups traveled westward to France, Holland, England, Germany, and the Spanish colonies in America. Some Jews and Moors in this western diaspora continued to practice their respective religions in the open and established synagogues and mosques in these new lands. Some converted genuinely to Protestantism in France, the Netherlands, and England, becoming Huguenots, Quakers, Lutherans, and even Presbyterians and Episcopalians.[2]

However, still others, especially those who immigrated to Spanish colonies in the Caribbean, South America, Mexico, and the United States, continued to practice their religion in secret, becoming crypto-Jews and crypto-Muslims.[3] In the American Southwest and in South America, as we will be discussing shortly, these crypto-Jews and Muslims maintained a surface appearance of being observant Catholics. Yet all the while, many families continued to practice Judaism and Islam in private, marrying only among themselves and confiding their "secret" to their children when they reached adolescence. Among the Melungeons, crypto-Judaism seemed to be the norm, with some family lines evolving over time into

---

[1]See Cecil Roth, *The Spanish Inquisition* (repr.: New York: W. W. Norton, 1964, 1996; c1937) 57-58.

[2]See Roth, *The Spanish Inquisition*, 163-83.

[3]See David Martin Gitlitz, *Secrecy and Deceit: The Religion of the Crypto-Jews*, Jewish Latin America series, intro. Ilan Stavans (Albuquerque: University of New Mexico Press, 2002; 1st ed.: Philadelphia: Jewish Publication Society, 1996).

full-fledged Christianity. However, among most Melungeon families, branches can also be found which openly practiced Judaism.

The central issue which I and several other Melungeon researchers struggle with at this date in the early twenty-first century is for how many generations Melungeons were aware of their Sephardic/Islamic identities and whether these religious traditions, which we still see among Primitive and Old Regular Baptists, were maintained out of conscious intent or simply force of habit. Certainly in my family and, for example, that of Brent Kennedy there was no attempt to communicate to our generation the Sephardic/Moorish origins of our ancestors. This knowledge has only come about through intensive, obsessive efforts to dig into an unwilling past. I do not believe my grandmother Carter was aware of her heritage, although she did know she was of "Black Dutch" ancestry. However, to her this may have meant she was "dark Dutch," not that she was Sephardic or Moor.

Perhaps my grandfather Carter—who had searched in vain for the "lost" silver treasure—did know, but if so, he never confided it to me or to his own children. However, when I married my husband, a Jewish man from New York City, my grandfather not only did not object to the match, but commented that "the Hebrews are a worthy people" and that I should "take pride in my husband's heritage." Odd words to have come from a Southern Appalachian Presbyterian, so perhaps somewhere/somehow he was aware that I was simply marrying one of my own, and his own, kind.[4] One of my most fervent wishes is that if such knowledge of our past is carried by any Melungeon descendants now living, they will be motivated by this book to come forward and tell the rest of us. How and by whom was this knowledge transmitted? Is it anywhere, in any form, written down, preserved or recorded? Perhaps we will never know.

Let us now consider other communities who are struggling with these same issues.

---

[4]I have subsequently learned from my mother that my grandfather Carter never ate pork or seafood and did not allow it to be served in their house. Thus, I am now even more certain that he was aware of his Jewish ancestry.

Colonies of Crypto-Jews

James R. Ross reports that colonies of Crypto-Jews have recently been "discovered" in Latin America, Spain, Portugal, New Mexico, and the Philippines—in fact, in virtually all those locales colonized by Spain. He notes that "in Brazil alone, there may be as many as fifteen million people—more than the entire world Jewish population—who descend from Iberian Jewish exiles." Those who continue to practice their beliefs are termed Marranos or Anusim and "have maintained their own culture and language within a closed circle for hundreds of years."[5]

Ross spent time with Marranos in Brazil and discovered fascinating details of their covert religion. For example, they worshipped together in their own parish "churches," which ostensibly were Catholic, but in fact were overseen by a fellow Marrano priest. Although baptisms and confessions were conducted, they were not taken seriously, but rather regarded as necessary performances to disguise their Jewish identity. Within their homes they lit candles on Friday at sunset and read passages from the Old Testament. They fasted during September to commemorate Yom Kippur, ate bitter herbs at Easter for Passover, and avoided pork and shellfish. Meat animals were slaughtered in kosher fashion, by cutting the neck and draining the blood.[6] True to their Sephardic origins, these Marranos also maintained Mediterranean superstitions as well. For example, they would say a special prayer to ward off nightmares and heal wounds, ask God to preserve them from the Evil Eye, and would vow, upon entering a church, that their adoration was reserved for the Eternal, rather than saints or icons.

Funeral rites among the Brazilian Marranos also followed Sephardic custom. They would wash the body of the deceased, wrap it in a linen shroud, place it in a coffin and bury the body the next day, with the feet facing eastward toward Jerusalem. A weeklong mourning period would be observed, during which all windows and mirrors were covered with

---

[5]James R. Ross, *Fragile Branches: Travels through the Jewish Diaspora* (New York: Riverhead Books, 2000; pbk. repr., 2001) 152.

[6]Interestingly, pigs are slaughtered in Melungeon areas of Appalachia in this same fashion—the throat is cut and then the carcass is hung by the hind legs to drain out all blood, which is discarded. The carcass is then rubbed with salt to remove any remaining blood.

black cloth. Some of these same customs were or are in use among the Melungeons.

Remarkable also is the existence of a secret group of Jewish persons termed *custudios* (custodians or caretakers) who had protected these Marranos since their arrival in Brazil during the 1500s. The custudios typically have prominent positions in the surrounding community and carefully guard their secret identities as Jews. Their task is to look out for the others and protect them from harm and harassment. I strongly suspect that attorneys Lewis Shepherd and John Netherland played this role for Melungeons during the 1800s, defending their interests in important ways, while keeping completely silent on their own Jewish heritage.[7] I similarly believe that Vardy Collins's "mineral springs resort" at Vardy, Tennessee was likely a mikveh, that is, a ritual Jewish bathing place, where Melungeons could go and practice their religion in private.

In many of the small, recently discovered crypto-Jewish communities, the members were unaware that other Jews still existed in the world. Perhaps the most romantic example of this was the discovery in 1917 of a community of several hundred Marranos in the tiny, north Portugal village of Belmonte. Convinced they were the only Jews left alive, they had carried on their faith in secret for five hundred years and knew only one remaining word in Hebrew—*Adonai*, "Lord." Significantly, this word was among those used as a first name among the Melungeon descendants whose genealogies I studied.[8]

An article by Eduardo Mayone Dias provides more details on the rural Portuguese crypto-Jewish experience.

> [D]uring the worst periods of persecution by the Inquisition, many of the Portuguese Jews forcibly converted to Catholicism in 1497 who

---

[7]John Netherland was an attorney in Rogersville, Tennessee who, in the mid-1800s, successfully brought a case to have Melungeons' voting rights restored. Although not classified as a Melungeon himself, his name, Netherland, and genealogy strongly suggest a Black Dutch/Sephardic origin. See *Ancestry and Descendants of Richard Netherland, Esq., 1764–1832,* in the Genealogical Room, Hawkins County Public Library.

[8]For example, The *Appalachian Quarterly* 2/3 (September 1997): 72, reports that the Allen Family of Clay County, Kentucky was founded by Job Allen and his brother *Adoniram*. A daughter of Adoniram was named Alie.

could not leave the country . . . may have sought refuge in mountainous areas on the northeastern strip of Portugal bordering Spain. . . .

Living among Christians, they had to give the appearance of following the same religion. Mosaic cult [Judaism] could only be observed in their homes under maximum secrecy. It was exclusively by means of a strict code, lasting even to our days, that the basic doctrine and tradition could be preserved in an underground fashion for approximately five hundred years. . . .

One of the first tactics to be adopted was abandonment of circumcision, since obviously any circumcised male falling prey to the so-called Holy Office would be immediately suspected of Judaizing. Also gone were all the writings in Hebrew (except medical texts) and all objects utilized in Jewish rituals, such as menorahs, mezuzahs, mizrahs, shofars, ceremonial knives used for circumcision, Torah covers, and talliths. (The tallith was sometimes replaced by a scarf with which *rezadeiras*, the female officiants that had taken the place of rabbis, covered their heads).

In order to compensate for the loss of sacred texts, some handwritten prayer books were compiled in later years. . . . Apart from these collections, the Old Testament was the only source of Jewish knowledge at the *conversos* disposal.

Ceremonies likely to attract public attention were forsaken. Thus celebrations such as Sukkoth, Rosh Hashanah, and Hanukkah ceased to be observed. Purim was celebrated for a time, but . . . it must have had an indoor character. Ritual killings of lambs and cattle were no longer publicly performed. The mikvah vanished from existence and old religious hymns were silenced. It appears that the practice of sweeping the house from the doorway into a room, rather than from inside out, often mentioned in the Inquisition proceedings, was eventually abandoned. (Also common among Sephardic groups in the Diaspora, its purpose is to avoid desecrating the mezuzah by sweeping the garbage past it.)[9] . . .

Jewish religious practices have been, up to present times, performed inside the house with doors and windows tightly closed. The Sabbath lamp was often placed at the bottom of a clay jar, so that the light could not be detected from outside. In the town of Braganca in the late 1920s, no child under twelve was taken to the meetings organized there for fear that in their innocence they would give away potentially dangerous information. . . .

---

[9]Consistent with this practice, my Grandmother Carter would tie her hair up in a white scarf every Friday afternoon and clean her entire house.

. . . [A]lthough the old practice of maintaining "Christian" first names (typically Catholic names, such as João or António, abound) is still in force, some crypto-Jews have chosen for their children such characteristically Jewish given names as Elias, Moises, Isajas, David, Daniel, Abraao, Ester, Sara, Raquel, Judite, Lia, or Anaisa. . . .

A long path of persecution has left its imprint on the minds of the Crypto-Jews up to our day and led to a haunting obsession with secrecy. . . . In 1991 a French TV crew was allowed to film the ceremony of the *matzoh* preparation for a documentary titled *Les Derniers Marranes* (*The Last Marranos*). Doors and windows had been securely closed. At a certain point in the documentary a knock at the door is heard, to which the participants react in absolute panic, notwithstanding the fact that the Inquisition had been abolished for some hundred and fifty years.[10]

"Melungeons" in the Southwest

I was on the internet looking up Sephardim and crypto-Jews when I came across references to what are likely our Melungeon "cousins," that is, very close kin, living in the American Southwest. During the 1980s several ethnographers, anthropologists, and folklorists began discovering communities of secret Jews living in New Mexico, Arizona, Colorado, and West Texas. These "Western Melungeons" had arrived around the same time as their Eastern colleagues—the mid 1500s—and for the same reasons. They had entered Spanish Mexico under the guise of being practicing Catholics and, once in America, had migrated to the far northern borders of La Mexico, just as the first Melungeons had migrated to the far northern regions of La Florida.

In these liminal borderlands there was less governmental supervision and, consequently, much less chance one would be identified by the Inquisition. Frances Hernandez writes of these people that

> Most of the Judaizers came after the Onate expedition, seeking refuge in New Mexico in the seventeenth century. . . .

---

[10]This long excerpt is from Eduardo Mayone Dias, "Crypto-Jews in Portugal—A Clandestine Existence," in *HaLapid*, journal/newsletter of the Society for Crypto-Judaic Studies (Winter 2000). The text appears also as a chapter in Dias's *Portugal's Secret Jews: The End of an Era* (Rumford RI: Peregrinação Publications, 1999).

In spite of the rigorous conditions, there was a distinct advantage for the secret Jews. Primarily, there were very few priests around. . . . No one was around to inquire about strange-sounding prayers, comment on over-frequent bathing in a land where there was usually a water shortage, or observe a suspicious repugnance for pork in communities where any kind of meat was rare. The secret Jews persevered unmolested in their isolated groups, completely out of touch with coreligionists anywhere in the world, but applying what they could recall of the law of Moses from generation to generation. Four hundred years after the New Christian Judaizers began to arrive in the upper Rio Grande Valley and its tributaries, there may be some 1,500 families within the wider Hispanic population who have legitimate claim to be their descendants. Their cognizance of this heritage ranges from the rare few who have a full understanding of their history and what it means, to those who have vague family references and realize that there are customs, taboos, and attitudes among their relatives that are unusual or unexplained, to those who have no comprehension of Judaism and their possible connection to it at all. . . .

Among the original settlers of San Gabriel, . . . are the following names that were recognized as usually Jewish: Caceres, Carrasco, Castro, Duran, Espinosa, Fernandez, Garcia, Gomez, Griego, Hernandez, Herrera, Ledesma, Leon, Lopez, Morales, Perez, Ramirez, Rivera, Robledo, Rodriguez, Romero, Sanchez, and Varela.[11]

Thus, here we see a pattern that closely parallels that of the Melungeons in the Southeast, that is, a set of intermarrying families carrying specific names and belonging to specific communities. And, concurrently, distinctive religious practices among these families that differ from those of the surrounding population. Further, as Hernandez comments, there was a strong tendency for first names among the Southwestern Crypto-Jews to be Hebrew, such as Esther, David, Abraham, Elias, Daniel, Isaac, Solomon, Sarah, Hannah, Rebecca, and Rachel, just as we find among the Melungeons. (In fact, Melungeon first names appear to be even more dis-

---

[11]Frances Hernandez, "The Secret Jews of the Southwest," in *Sephardim in the Americas: Studies in Culture and History*, ed. Martin A. Cohen and Abraham J. Peck, Judaic Studies Series (Tuscaloosa and London: American Jewish Archives and University of Alabama Press, 1993) 414. (Or see Hernandez's original article in the *American Jewish Archives Journal* 44 (1992): 411-54.)

tinctively Hebrew and Mediterranean, for example, Ramon, Naomi, Herschel, Allafair, Aliyah, Miriam.) Hernandez further notes that

> Endogamous marriage has probably been the most critical of the measures taken to maintain this culture in the hinterlands. Researchers are mapping the patterns of intermarriage, finding frequent connections through many generations of the Espinosas, Villanuevas, Castros, Atencios, Carrascos, Gomezes, Luceros, and Lopezes. Although Dennis Duran was not apprised of his Jewish heritage while he was growing up, his mother made clear to him that he must select his wife from a list of specific families.[12]

Regarding the Melungeons, we see similar intramarriage patterns among the Collins, Gibsons, Goens, Hales, Addingtons, Mullins, Carricos, and so forth. This is why, even 400 years later, DNA studies find such a consistent and distinctive Sephardic/Moorish genetic pattern.

---

[12]Hernandez, "The Secret Jews of the Southwest," 437.

Further, just as the Melungeons tended to be buried in given cemeteries with given markers, so also did the Southwestern Crypto-Jews.[13] Hernandez writes that

> Burial usually took place in the local Catholic cemetery. . . . But areas of the *camposanto* were set aside for individual groups of relatives. In some of these sections the headstones all face east and are blank except for the names and dates of the deceased. In some locales, . . . gravestones can be uncovered in the underbrush that have stars of David and menorahs carved on them. . . . In many cemeteries, markers can be found with both Jewish and Christian symbols, or occasionally the Masonic symbol as well.

Emilio and Trudi Coca of Santa Fe have produced an extensive photographic study of these revealing stones, comparing them to pic-

---

[13]For example, examination of Fannie Lane Steele and Ina Jean Stanley Dotson, *The Crabtree-Stanley Collection: A Collection of the Ancestry and Descendants of James Crabtree and James Stanley* (Midland VA: I. J. S. Dotson, 1996) suggests that these families are of Sephardic/Melungeon ancestry, e.g., Jacob Crabtree married Mary Price 1786, lived in Lee County, Virginia, and had five children: Job, Richard, Hannah, Sarah and Rebeccah (12). The Crabtrees intermarried with the Mullins family and had children named Cohen Mullins and Joel Leon Mullins (71). There was also intermarriage with Daniel Silva, son of Frank and Mary Gomes Silva. Many members of both the Dotson and Crabtree families were Primitive and Old Regular Baptist Church members, and given names include many of Hebrew origin, e.g., Abraham, Shadrack, Jesse, Moses, Amelia, Nathan, Abigail, Isaac, Daniel, Lot, Susannah, Sarah, Jacob, and Sinai (601).

Nancy Clark Brown and Rhonda Robertson, in *The Addingtons of Virginia: The Descendants of William Addington and Margaret Cromwell* (Wise VA: Sainte Marie on the Clinch, 1994) suggest a strong Sephardic/Moorish/Melungeon component in this family and its related lines as well. The families ventured to Southwest Virginia during the same time as the great Melungeon migration (1770–1810) and lived among several Melungeon families. Several family members belonged to the Stoney Creek Primitive Baptist Church. A daughter is named Allah (416). A male family member was a Mason and had a Masonic symbol on his gravestone (G. W. Stallard, Scott County, Virginia, 624). Other Stallards (692, 641) married into the Jacobs and Carrico families (650). The related Cromwell family appears to have Sephardic origins and to have migrated to Virginia from Baltimore (813). Remarkably, one of the female Cromwells appears to have married the Christopher Gist who scouted the Southwest Virginia frontier (811).

tures of stones with similar designs in authentic Jewish cemeteries in other parts of the country. In the old Penitente cemetery at Santa Rosa, for example, . . . they found etched beneath the standard crosses clear outlines of stars of David, menorahs, six-petaled flowers, hands with fingers spread to form six groupings—all Judaic symbols recognizable to the initiated. Michael Atlas Acuna of Pueblo, Colorado, has found Hispanic Catholic cemeteries in that area where stones are decorated with stars of David, eternal lights, and six-point lilies. He also reports that in a 170-year-old rural church near Trinidad, one can see stars of David with "Adonai" inscribed in the centers, menorahs, and the Ten Commandments in Hebrew all worked into the stained-glass windows.[14]

Not surprisingly, here we encounter the Freemasons as well. Hernandez further reports that

A second connection for some communities has been the Masonic lodges. . . . Gravestones in the cemeteries at Monticello, Anton Chico, Bernal, San Marcial, and Tecolote feature Masonic symbols, sometimes along with disguised Jewish signs. On a few markers in the separate graveyards around Puerta de Luna, the Masonic symbols bear Hebrew inscriptions within them.[15]

For the Melungeons dwelling in the southeastern Appalachians the discovery of ethnic kin in the American Southwest should be good news. We are not alone; there are others like ourselves. Like finding a sibling one never knew existed, there is now the opportunity not only to reclaim our heritage, but also to participate in an extended family—one that has had a long and traumatic, but brilliant, past and which can now go about the business of constructing an identity to take into the future.

---

[14]Hernandez, "The Secret Jews of the Southwest," 432.
[15]Hernandez, "The Secret Jews of the Southwest," 432.

Chapter 9

Reconstructing Our Past and Exploring Our Future: Whither The Melungeons?

There probably are many pieces of Melungeon culture still present (or lasting until the recent past) waiting to be identified. It is vitally important to collect and catalog these so we and future generations will have a record of ourselves. Architecture, recipes, apparel, religious practices, mythology, musical preferences, language, superstitions, dances, stories, and recreational pastimes are all part of the cultural heritage that could and should be a significant part of our and America's history. In pursuit of these cultural remnants, I scoured the available books by, for, or about Melungeons and sent out a questionnaire on nine cultural dimensions (ranging from apparel practices to gender roles) to 143 persons subscribing to Bill Fields's Melungeon newsletter, *Under One Sky*.[1] Here is what I learned.

Apparel. Melungeon women often wore floor-length, long sleeved, high-necked black dresses. Some also wore headscarves, while others wore handmade bonnets covering their hair. Women's hair was kept long and often braided and wrapped around the crown of the head or parted in the middle and worn pulled back in a bun. Photos of my own family show the women dressed in this fashion, as do several others, as well.

Men often wore suits, complete with hats, and full beards or mustaches. These apparel styles appear to be Sephardic/Moorish in origin

---

[1] *Under One Sky. The Melungeon Information Exchange* "was a printed newsletter dedicated to research into the history, genealogy, and origins of the Melungeons and other mixed-race people." The newsletter was published from 1995 to 2000 and distributed free of charge. A website remains, with links to some articles from the newsletter and to other sites of interest: <http://www.underonesky.org/Under_One_Sky.html>.

and are different from those found among the Scotch-Irish and English. One respondent reported that Melungeon men occasionally wore turban-like head wraps, with waist sashes.[2]

Others reported that Melungeon women and children often went barefoot and could walk long distances without shoes.

Food and Food Preparation. The Middle Eastern influence was clearly evident in Melungeon food practices. Some groups, especially those living near Wise, Virginia, were so fond of seasoning food with wild onions that they were called "ramps" for a local wild leek. Several sources also report the Melungeon fondness for wild greens, "sallet," which was often eaten with corn bread. Dried foods included various kinds of beans and peppers. Additionally, peppers, onions, cumin, mace, poppy seeds, coriander, and garlic were frequently used as seasonings. Tomato sauces and gravies, tripe, and various types of "flat" (Semitic) bread were also mentioned by several Melungeon descendants. Fried pies containing fruit and/or meat and/or vegetables were also common. These echo foods eaten by crypto-Jews in the Southwest.

> They fried *empanada*, small pastries filled with pumpkin, or what-ever dried, spiced vegetables were left from the winter hoard. Some-times the triangular pies were referred to as hamantashin ("Haman's hat"). These pies were consumed with much drinking and singing by neighbors dressed up in their new spring clothes. . . .
> [During] April, when the Spanish villages were busy with their passionate celebration of Easter, some families were repeating their own different customs related to the season. Dennis Duran recalls that his people baked unleavened bread for several spring days, which the chil-dren looked forward to because of its surprising crispness. Other special foods marked that week: *sopa*, a bread pudding with cinnamon and raisins, *capirotada*, layers of bread, dried fruit, cheese and syrup baked together as a festive dessert; and the *lentajas*, or pastries, cooked with venison. The Saturday before Easter, the men prepared a large salad, featuring the earliest vegetables in the spring garden, and that was all that the families ate until sundown. On Good Friday, *tortas de huevo* were the only food served: thick slices of potato dipped in egg batter and fried in hot chile sauce. To celebrate the holy Sunday, all groups,

---

[2]Two respondents reported that Melungeon women wore *bright* colors, bright glass and gold jewelry and bright scarves/shawls. These persons may be of Moorish or Gypsy descent.

both Catholic and suspect Catholic, baked or roasted whole kids, *cabritos*, in underground ember pits. But certain families drained blood from the slaughtered animals and used it to mark unobtrusive signs on their doors.[3]

Similar Melungeon dishes include breaded fried tomatoes, hominy, black-eyed peas, okra, yellow squash and zucchini, chicken and dumplings, oats fried with brown sugar, rice and bread pudding, cornbread and beans with onions, cornbread mixed with buttermilk (which my grandfather ate regularly), fried chicken, tomato dumplings and, remarkably, what is actually a Spanish molé-sauce, but called by the Melungeons "chocolate gravy," which is poured over various breads. Melungeons also reportedly liked raisins, pumpkin pie, biscuits, and sweet grape wines.[4]

Melungeons, true to their Middle-Eastern and Spanish heritage, also preferred *coffee* over tea. (Legend has it that "coffee" was discovered by an Ethiopian goatherd, then first cultivated by other Arabs on the Arab Peninsula to make "gahwa.") And I suspect that "red-eye" gravy, which consists of pepper, onions, pork drippings, and coffee is of Melungeon origin. Cooked rice, cream, butter, and sugar mixed together were also popular for breakfast. (My grandmother often served this to my brother and me on our visits to her house.)

Music. Apparently, the "mountain dulcimer" is of Melungeon origin, being developed in Persia and played by Sephardic Jews and Moors. This would make sense, as use of the dulcimer in the United States is confined almost exclusively to the remote Appalachian regions where the Melungeons settled. Conversely, the more widely used fiddle, guitar, and banjo were brought over by the Scotch-Irish, English, and Africans, and are much more widely in use.

The other type of music which I believe is likely uniquely Melungeon in origin is the a cappella "lining" of songs performed in the Primitive and Old Regular Baptist churches. This singing style likely originated

---

[3]Frances Hernandez, "The Secret Jews of the Southwest," *American Jewish Archives* 44 (1992): 49-50.

[4]Paul M. Fink, in *Jonesborough: The First Century of Tennessee's First Town, 1776–1876*, 2nd ed. (Johnson City TN: Overmountain Press, 1989) 57, also reports that the early inhabitants of Jonesborough produced ample quantities of brandy, a Mediterranean drink, most of which was consumed locally.

with Sephardic cantors. It cannot be attributed to the African, Scotch-Irish, or English settlers.

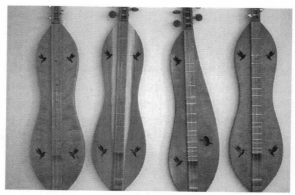

Dulcimers.

Ginseng.

Herbs, Folk Medicines, and Magic. Virtually all commentators on Melungeons have noted their facility in using herbs as folk medicines and their deep knowledge of wild plant growth patterns and locations. Perhaps the herb most often associated with them is *ginseng*, a root which grows wild in the Appalachians and is much prized by Chinese consumers as a remedy. Bonnie Ball, for example, writes that

> After crops were "laid by" . . . the men and older boys would get together a shotgun or two, some corn meal, coffee, bacon, lots of tobacco, knives, pails, a frying pan, and possibly an oil lantern. Thus outfitted, they would take to the hills and ridges for a week's expedition of digging ginseng [for the market]. Their travels often took them into the more remote areas of Stone Mountain, where the location of the prized ginseng was a carefully guarded secret. They slept under cliffs and ledges, killed and ate small game, and generally "lived off the land."[5]

When I was looking up ginseng on the internet to learn more about its history and medicinal properties, I came across a remarkable fact. One of the first known gatherers and sellers of the root was *Daniel Boone*, who we now know to be of likely Sephardic descent. Boone would gather huge quantities of the herb and ship it from Richmond, Virginia to China. What interested me about this was not only that Boone engaged in such trading activity, but that a supposedly uneducated man who had never traveled out of the country, much less to China, would even be aware that ginseng existed and that a valuable market was available for it in China.

Further investigation revealed that the Chinese demand for ginseng had originated in the *sixteenth century*, coinciding with the Spanish exploration of the Americas, including of course, Santa Elena and Juan Pardo's expeditions into the interior of the southeastern United States. We know from the excavations at Santa Elena that the settlers there were engaged in trade with China,[6] and had already gained knowledge of several native plants and herbs (for example, tobacco and corn) from the Indians.

---

[5]Bonie Sage Ball, *The Melungeons: Notes on the Origin of a Race*, rev. ed. (Johnson City TN: Overmountain Press, 1992) 85-86.

[6]Stanley A. South, *Archæology at Santa Elena: Doorway to the Past* (Columbia: South Carolina Institute of Archaeology and Anthropology, 1991).

What I now believe is that a trade in ginseng was established with China by the Sephardic Spanish settlers at Santa Elena and that later Sephardic immigrants to Appalachia simply continued (or reestablished) this trade pattern.[7] If my line of reasoning is correct, it would also tie in nicely with the "Swift's Silver Mine" legends which originated at the same time as Boone's ventures. Careful investigation, I believe, will show well-established, and likely illegal, trade patterns into and out of the Appalachians via the Sephardi-Moor-Freemason-Barbary pirate shipping routes.

Religion. The Sephardic Jews and Berber Moors who made up the bulk of Melungeon population were never far removed from *animism*—the belief that spirits inhabited all aspects of the natural world. (For that matter, neither were the Scotch-Irish Celts.) Prior to the advent of monotheism, the Semitic and North African peoples viewed lunar and solar powers as paramount in their lives.[8] Thus, it is not surprising that in the raw and natural wilderness of Appalachia, these dormant religious impulses would reassert themselves. Jesse Stuart, in his novel *Daughter of the Legend*, notes that

> All the Melungeons believed the moon had a great influence on their lives. Every Melungeon shack on the mountain had an almanac, and if the Melungeon could read, he went by the signs. If no one in the family could read, he had somebody read the almanac for him. The moon had the greatest influence on Melungeon life, and next came the sun and then the wind. When I rove the clapboards to roof our cabin, I was told I was doing it right for I was doing it in the dark of the moon, which meant they would never curl up on the cabin roof in the summer sun. The sun was [seen as] a great source of light and warmth that made plants grow. The sun was a mother to all vegetable life. How many times have I heard that "the eye of the sun is upon us." They talk about the sun as if it was a great powerful god in the sky looking down upon their crops, their timbered lands, and upon them. The wind was something that carried them messages. The wind told a Melungeon

---

[7]Otherwise, we are hard pressed to explain why intrepid explorer Daniel Boone stumbled across a ginseng root one day in the forest and thought to himself, "Hey, I'll bet the Chinese would love this stuff. I'll dig up several tons and ship it over there!"

[8]Michael Brett and Elizabeth Fentress, *The Berbers* (Malden MA and Oxford UK: Blackwell, 2002).

when there would be rain and how much rain to expect. The wind told him when there would be frost and snow. It warned him not to plant too soon else his good seeds would lie in the cold ground and never sprout.[9]

My survey of Melungeon descendants yielded some other interesting beliefs and superstitions.

•Throwing a silver coin into a baby boy's first bath water for good luck and fortune.
•Crops were planted and butchering done according to lunar signs.
•Astrological signs and dreams were interpreted as to their meaning for the future.
•If there were frequent twin births, this was seen as a message from the spirit world.
•Division of animals into hooved and clawed.
•Witches, ghosts, and "haunts" existed. A witch could cast an evil eye curse on a newborn.
•The future could be read in coffee grounds, animal entrails, and cloud formations.
•Numerology of one's name (gematria).
•It was considered good luck for visitors to bring gifts, especially to children.
•Signs such as six pointed stars, hexagrams, and other symbols would be put on overhead doorframes using nails or by carving.
•Ghosts could enter the house and make noises; they could arise from the graveyard at night and roam the countryside. One could leave bread and milk for them to eat.
•Rituals existed which could be used to remove warts, cure thrush, and stop bleeding.
•A divining rod or "water witch"—a forked stick made from a peach tree limb—could be used to find water for wells.
•Not only should the house be swept clean daily, but also the path from the front steps to the road and occasionally, the entire yard would be swept. (This was definitely *not* a Scotch-Irish practice.)
•Once a year, new sand was spread on the cabin floor and front yard.

Housing and Architecture. Because of their Mediterranean origins, the Melungeons have carried forward some unique architectural traditions. Perhaps the most commonly cited are the use of *arched* doorways and windows. Rounded porches (porticoes) and interior rooms were also

---

[9]Jesse Stuart, *Daughter of the Legend* (New York: McGraw-Hill, 1965) 215.

mentioned by my respondents. These features likely are drawn from their Moorish heritage and—on a much simpler level—reflect architectural marvels such as the Alhambra in Spain.

I also learned from my informants that Melungeon households typically had flowerbeds around the exterior of the house; these frequently contained calla lilies, snapdragons, and violets. This also is typical of Spanish, Moorish, and Sephardic culture, but atypical among the Scotch-Irish, who had cosettled the Appalachians.

Melungeon vegetable gardens also featured more emphasis on squash, tomatoes, beans, peppers, onions, and radishes than those the Scotch-Irish raised. The Scotch-Irish diet in Appalachia was more oriented toward carrots, potatoes, and corn.

Burial and Mourning Customs. Some description of Melungeon burial practices was given in chapter 7; however, the respondents to the survey provided additional information, which is included here. There was a split among my respondents in terms of the time reported from death to burial, with about half saying burial occurred within one day, the rest reporting three days. Among Moslems and Jews, burial occurs within one day; thus the three-day practice among some Melungeon families was likely adopted from their Scotch-Irish neighbors.

Respondents also differed regarding grave markers. Some mentioned "regular" vertical, engraved headstones (a Scotch-Irish practice), while others reported flat headstones or footstones (a Judaic Sephardic practice), while still others stated that no markers were used. "Decoration Day," the ritual of putting flowers on ancestors' graves in spring or summer, together with a large family feast and gathering in the cemetery, appears derived from Sephardic and Moorish practice, as is the year-long mourning period.

Into the Future

For generations the Appalachian people known as Melungeons carried on their lives and traditions uncertain both as to who their ancestors really were and from where, exactly, their rituals had come. All the while they were surrounded by others who were "whiter," stronger, and often ready to repress and dominate them. Although early Melungeon settlers were well aware of what they were *not*—that is, *not* Scotch-Irish, *not* English, *not* German, *not* French, *not* Negro—few of the present generation were/are aware of what they *are*: the descendants of Sephardic Jews and

Muslim Moors who likely first arrived on North American shores during the 1500s and continued to increase their numbers through births and in-migration through the 1600s and 1700s.

It is indeed a stunning revision of American history to think that the earliest settlers in Virginia, West Virginia, North Carolina, Georgia, South Carolina, Florida, Kentucky, and Tennessee were not stalwart, white-skinned Anglo-Saxons and Celts from the British Isles, but rather dusky, dark-eyed, dark haired, exotic, non-Christian Sephardim and Berbers from North Africa and Spain. It was Moors who occupied (John) Blackmore's (Black-a-moor's) Fort on the Clinch River. It was a Sephardic Daniel Boone who cleared the path through the Cumberland Gap into Kentucky. This knowledge challenges not only our view of American history, but also the modern image of Jews and Muslims.

How ironic to think that these two peoples, whom we usually hear about shooting each other on the West Bank and Gaza Strip, were—450 years ago—trudging together inland toward the Appalachian Mountains. Intermarrying, reproducing, becoming Primitive and Old Regular Baptists, going to Freemason meetings, riding horses, shooting rifles, salting hogs, growing corn and tobacco, fighting the British at King's Mountain, and fighting both the Yankees and the Rebels during the Civil War. It makes us realize how enormously adaptive and creative they must have been, how strong their will to survive.

My own family histories show an interweaving of Muslim and Jewish names: Mecca and Sarah, Aliyah and Rachel, Omar Ishmael and Reuben Abraham. Refugees from the Inquisition, they became comrades in arms, trading partners, marriage partners, pioneers, farmers, soldiers, mothers and fathers.

I am at a loss to augur what the future will bring. It has been only four years since I first learned of my own Melungeon identity. I haven't yet worked out what to make of it. What I am motivated to do—as I suspect are many others in the same position—is to demand a greater accountability regarding our past. To paraphrase the infamous Watergate Senate hearings: Who knew about us and when did they know it? Or perhaps more accurately: When did they stop knowing it? When and how were the decisions made to bury our heritage? Was the pressure of the Ku Klux Klan too great to continue even a clandestine Jewish/Muslim identity? Was there a particular generation that simply decided to "give it up"—maybe in 1850 or 1890 or 1920?

I am angry about this—me in my formerly privileged, white, Protestant, professionalism. I want to find that vault where the secrets lie buried and break into it. What would the secrets look like? What would they say? Like the lost Swift Silver Mines, the answers lie in some once known but now forgotten hills in Appalachia. Maybe if enough of us go seeking them, they will be discovered.

Some Closing Thoughts on Race, Religion, and Ethnicity

In my academic research I have often studied issues of race, religion, and ethnicity as they pertained to consumer behavior. However, I was always able to do this from the perspective of a "privileged observer." My presumed status (now, of course, known to be incorrect) as a white, Anglo-Saxon, Protestant woman of aristocratic bloodlines permitted me to stand apart from (and above) the ethnic and racial fray. I could exercise my egalitarian and liberal judgments about downtrodden minorities from the secure perch of privilege.

Now that I find myself included among the "mongrels," "barbarians," and "off-scourings of the Earth," my view has changed—but not completely. While certainly there is ample evidence to support the notion that some Melungeons—and especially those who were publicly *labeled* as Melungeons—were subjected to racial bigotry and political, social, and economic repression,[10] the Melungeon population as a whole did *not* constitute an "oppressed" or "underprivileged" minority, as some have recently claimed. This is even more true for their descendants; especially the past three or four generations, the vast majority of whom were not even aware that they were/are "Melungeons"! Indeed, most present-day persons of Melungeon descent have always believed—and been so perceived by others—that they were white, Scotch-Irish and/or English, and Protestant.

It is important to recognize that this belief and perception prevailed, despite the fact that many persons of Melungeon descent (such as myself, my mother, my father, and my grandmother Carter) are tangibly darker than persons of actual British descent. In fact, one fascinating example of the ability of racial/ethnic perceptions to override racial/ethnic physical appearance is that while I was attending Dobyns-Bennett High School in

---

[10]See especially Kennedy, *The Melungeons*.

Kingsport, Tennessee there were two girls in the same class as I, who *were* known to be of Syrian and Lebanese ancestry, respectively. These two girls, who I will call Frances and Jane, were quite close in appearance to me in terms of skin color, hair color and texture, eye color, and facial features. Yet because they were known to be "Semitic" or "Middle Eastern," they were viewed as exotic and therefore pretty much off-limits as far as dating was concerned. They were not classified as "not-like-us: bad" as Negroes were when our schools were integrated, but rather as "not-like-us: strange/unusual." Both, I am sure, were thrilled when they graduated and were able to move away to more multicultural environments.

In her book *Suddenly Jewish*, Barbara Kessel describes instances in which people, most often adults, have discovered (much as I did) that they are actually of Jewish descent.[11] They often then reexamine their lives and family traditions and discover that the evidence of their Hebrew origins was all around them, they just didn't "see" it. In one poignant anecdote, Kessel relates how a young woman's grandmother took her to visit her great uncle (the grandmother's brother) whom the young woman had never met before and, in fact, did not even know existed. The great uncle was in a nursing home and dying. His last name, unlike the grandmother's, was distinctly Jewish. When the young woman saw him, she thought to herself, "He looks just like an old Jewish man." She then realized that the man also looked just like her beloved grandmother. "But he's Jewish!" exclaimed the young woman. "Yes, and so am *I*, and so are *you*," replied the grandmother. Truth often hides in plain sight.

Because most modern-day Melungeons were not and are not labeled as "colored people" or as "Jews" or "Muslims," they have not suffered the abuses commonly heaped upon these groups. I do not believe we are a victimized minority group. In the past, *some* of our Melungeon ancestors were mistreated, harassed, and even killed. But *we*, the present generation, are distantly removed from this and to position ourselves as racially persecuted is simply wrong.

Analogously, we were *not* formed as a haphazard collection of racial and/or religious castoffs. True, as Sephardic Jews and Muslims we were

---

[11]Barbara Kessel, *Suddenly Jewish: Jews Raised as Gentiles Discover Their Jewish Roots*, Brandeis Series in American Jewish History, Culture, and Life (Hanover NH: University Press of New England, 2000).

pursued to the ends of the earth (literally) by the Inquisition; but, as the foregoing analysis has shown, once our ancestors arrived on *these* shores and walked, rode, swam, or ran to *these* mountains, they were "home free." Watauga Country, the Holston Settlement, the Nolichucky Settlement, Boonesborough, Kentucky, and Wise County, Virginia were "ours." Melungeons ran the government, established the stores and newspapers, owned the land, distilled the brandy, shipped the corn and tobacco, set up the houses of worship, forged the iron, and formed the militia. Importantly, over a fifty-year period (1770–1820), new settlers were actively recruited from among our own kind. Wagonloads of Sephards and Moors converged on Melungeon settlements from along the Eastern Seaboard. They purposely married one another and (apparently with great vigor) produced thousands more "Melungeons." Further, they constructed and maintained their own culture, apart from that of their Scotch-Irish and English neighbors. It is in revitalizing (or as cousin Brent would put it, resurrecting) this culture that our ethnic future lies. Let's get going!

Appendixes

Appendix 1
Surnames of Probable Melungeon Descent

Below is a list of names (taken from Kennedy) considered to be of Melungeon descent.[1] Some of these names are also common to Scotch-Irish, English, Welsh, and German immigrants to the United States and those carrying them could possibly have no Melungeon connection. However, *if* the persons carrying them were living in the Appalachian areas populated by Melungeons during the 1600s, 1700s, and 1800s, then the probability of Melungeon descent is high. Genealogical research has shown a high degree of intermarriage among families having these surnames within Melungeon populated areas. To determine if a given individual *is* of Melungeon descent, genealogical and DNA analyses should be conducted.

Adams	Bass	Bowman
Adkins	Beckler	Branham
Allen	Bell	Braveboy
Alley	Bennett	Briger/Bridger
Allmond	Berry	Brogan
Ashe	Beverly	Brooks
Ashworth	Biggs	Brown
Barker	Bolen/Bowlen/Bowlin	Bullion
Barnes	Boone	Bunch

---

[1]This list is a combination of the several categorical lists of "Common Melungeon and Related Surnames" in N. Brent Kennedy and Robyn Vaughan Kennedy, *The Melungeons. The Resurrection of a Proud People. An Untold Story of Ethnic Cleansing in America*, 2nd rev. and corr. ed. (Macon GA: Mercer University Press, 1997) 171-74.

Burton
Butler
Buxton
Campbell
Carrico/Carico
Carter
Casteel/Cassell/Castle
Caudill
Chapman/Chafin/Chaffin
Chavis/Chaves
Clark
Cloud
Coal/Cole/Coles
Coffey
Coleman
Colley
Collier/Colyer
Collins
Collinsworth
Cook(e)
Cooper
Cotman
Counts
Cox/Coxe
Criel
Crow
Cumba/Cumbo
Cumba/CumboJackson
Curry/Khourie
Custalow
Dalton
Dare
Davis
Denham
Dennis
Dial
Dorton
Doyle
Driggers
Dye
Ely
Epps

Evans
Fields
Freeman
French
Gann
Garland
Gibbs
Gibson/Gipson
Goins/Goings
Gorvens
Gowan/Gowen
Graham
Green(e)
Gwinn/Gwynn
Hall/Hale/Haile
Hammon
Harmon
Harris
Harvie/Harvey
Hawkes
Hendricks/Hendrix
Hill
Hillman
Hogge
Holmes
Hopkins
Howe
Hyatt
James
Johnson
Jones/Jonas
Keith
Kennedy
Kiser
Langston
Lasie
Lawson
Locklear
Lopes/Lopez
Lowry
Lucas
Maddox

Maggard
Major
Male/Mayle
Malony
Marsh
Martin
Miles
Minard
Miner/Minor
Mizer
Moore
Morley
Mullins
Nash
Nelson
Newman
Niccans
Nichols
Noel
Norris
Orr
Osborn/Osborne
Oxendine
Page
Paine
Patterson
Perkins
Perry
Phelps
Phipps
Polly
Powell
Powers
Prinder
Pritchard
Pruit
Ramey
Rasnick/Rasnake
Reaves/Reeves
Revels
Richardson
Roberson/Robertson

Robinson
Russell
Sammons
Sampson
Sawyer
Scott
Sexton
Shavis
Shepard/Shepherd
Short/Shortt
Sizemore
Smiling
Smith
Stallard
Stanley

Steel
Stewart
Strother
Sweatt/Swett
Swindall
Tally
Taylor
Thompson
Tolliver/Taliafero
Tuppance
Turner
Vanover
Vicars/Viccars/Vickers
Ware
Watts

Weaver
White
Whited
Wilkins
Williams
Williamson
Willis
Wisby
Wise
Wolf(e)
Wood
Wright
Wyatt
Wynn

Appendix 2
Carter Family: Melungeon Given Names

The names listed below are taken from my own Carter ancestry in South-west Virginia.[2] This family's history is discussed in chapter 5 and passim.

Genoa Dove	Elva	Tabitha	Coroia
Marcus	Leonidus	Serena	Emanuel
Cassey (M)	Desinda	Lydia Drucilla	Reuben
Naomi	Mosco	Louisa Melpha	Pennetia
Alma Vera	Vinetta	Miriam	Mogella
Echol (M)	Leroy	Ferdinand	Mariah
Cena	Lenora	Jaelia	Rintha
Altamissa	Drushana	Bouria	Lavinia
Cozza	Herschel	Lathan	Dovie
Israel	Callie	Aurelia	Sciota
Letha	Jemima	Locado	Mecca
Keziah	Sefronia	Caleb	Elkanah
Didama	Derinda	Rachel	Emeretta
Sarida	Lolla	Nevada	Myhr
Judah	Allie	Darthula	Asseline
Isaac	Arlie	Abram	Caldonia
Serapta	Osta	Avonia	Mossia
Marguerite	Lorenzo	Viola	Delpha
Nila	Rosanna	Neniva	Jaeley
Alvena	Juanita	Elvira	Isham
Fonso	Isabella	Ephraim	Isabelle
Flavius	Delila	Elijah	Colohagh
Charmie	Rhoda Launa	Nathan	Sina
Nannie	Myrtle Mae	Oberia	Orpha
Disa	Angelina	Zion	Jobe
Zouria	Elva	Vestine	Buena Vista
Lemuel	Moses	Cuva	Dora
FloraRico	Arminda	Saluda	Delmus
Dicey	Lapluma	Ardemia	Lovella
Onia	Carmen	Minda	Rosa

---

[2]Compiled from Rita K. Sutton, *Early Carters in Scott County, Virginia* (N.p.: R. K. Sutton, 1981, 1983).

Lula
Orlena
Minerva
Alba
Didana
Louisiana
Valentine (M)
Ruhaney
Alta
Lucinda
Siala
Montavia

Ollie May
Arabella
Josiah
Solomon
Arreny
Fernando
Barilla
Tempa
Mahala
Hezekiah
Nimrod
Ephraim

Flavily
Rosabecca
Saphronia
Ophelia
Artemissa
Atalla
Idella
Carmen
Sedonia
Minnia Rosa
Basil
Tennie

Sebastian
Sylvan
Desha
Louemma
Evada
Ramona
Mariah
Obijah
Nicatie
Palistine

Appendix 3
Purrysburgh Colony, Beaufort County, S.C. 1743[3]

Buch	Ulrich		Chiviller	John	
Bucke	Abram		Choupart	Daniel	
	Daniel Henry		Christian	David	
	Francis		Cl Croix	Alexander	
	Francois		Cobley	Jennett	
	Jean Pierre		Collume	Jacob	
	Margarette		Coste	Issac	
	Susanne		Cronenberger	Nicolas	
	David			Henrich	
Bugnion	Mr.		Cuillat	Adam	
Brickell	Christopher			Wallier	
Brulott	Mons. Guill		Da Roch	John Henry	
Bourquin	Mary		Dalescale	Vincent	
Boyer	Jeanne	Urbseine	De Beufin	Hector B.	
Babant	John		De Gallier	Jean Henry	
Brace	John	Peter	De Gallin	Jean Pierre	
Breton	Francoise		De Jeau	Capt.	
	Jean	Pierre	De Las	James	
Bourguin	Henry		De Mon Clar	Andre	
	Henry	Francoise	De Pia	Peter	
	Jean	Baptist	De La Gaye	John	
	John		De Lane	Samuel	
Butla	Monseiur		Del Pont	Jean	
Calane	Jacob		Derich	John Henry	
Calis	Benjamin		De Saussure	Henry	
Chardonet	Abraham		Det Meshe	Peter	
Charmason	Peter		Detrevid	Godfrey	
Chefeille	Henry		Detpcher	Peter	
Chevelis	John		Devall	Louis	

---

[3]This list is taken from Paul R. Sarrett, Jr. (e-mail: <prsjr@aol.com>) at <http://ftp.rootsweb.com/pub/usgenweb/sc/sccolony.txt>. This may be the "large arrival of persons of Cathaginian descent" to South Carolina referred to by Lewis Shepherd in the Chattanooga Melungeon trial. Their colony was located within a few miles of the original Santa Elena colony of 1567–1587. Founded in the 1700s ostensibly by Swiss Protestant colonists, the names listed suggest that Purrysburgh was in fact a cryto-Jewish community. Virtually all the names appear on lists of Sephardic Jews. See, for example, <www.sephardim.com>.

Devill	Lewis		Abraham
De Vision	Peter Abraham		Daniel
Donnatt	Abraham		Marguerite
Dorff	George Minguers	Humber	David Pierre
Duberdosser	Henry	Huquin	David
Ecolier	David	Ingler	Anna
Egnia	Ann Marie	Isoug(Issac)	Hans Ulrick
Elizabeth	Eve	Jacot	Susanne
Elizard	Abraham	Jeanneret	Pierre
Enderlin	Henry		Anne
Fallet	Abraham	Jenbuch	John
Fauconet	David	Jindra	Abraham
Faure	Francois	Jouse	Abram Jacques
Flar	Mons.		Henry
Flower	Joseph Edward		Jean Pierre
Fountain	John	Justin	Eliasor
Franck	Leonard	Kehl	Lewis
	Daniel	Khell	Loudwick
	Ann Barbara	Kneffer	David
Galache	Pierre	Kohl	Luis
Gantier	David	La Pierre	Matthew
Gasman	Henry	La Bord	John
Genbretz	John	Laffite	Peter
Geroud	David	La Gayes	John
Girardin	Anne	Lasman	John Martin
	David	Laye	Joseph
	Henry	Le Roy	Abraham
	Jean Henry	La Gare	John
	Joseph	Lier	John
Goliere	Anthony	Linder	John
Gombze	Michael	Lutle	Peter
Grabs	John	Madeleine	Marid
Grand	John Rodolph	Maillier	Peter
Grenier	John	Malkey	Abraham
Grob	Andelheith	Mallett	Gideon
	Elizabeth	Malliet	Pierre
Grober	George S.	Margarita	Anna
Grovenberg	Henry		Maria
Henrie	Mary		Elizabeth
Henriond	Benjamin	Marill	Anna
Henry	John Francis	Marte	Abram
Herchnecht	George	Masson	Mary
Holzendorf	John		Peter
Huginier/		Mattey	Abraham
Huguenin/		Mayorholtser	John Henry
Huguenium	David	Mefgersdoff	Hendrick

	Sorg		Nicholas
Merret	Daniel	Ring	John
	John Philip	Roche	Jacob
Metsger	Jacob		Henry
Meuron	Abram Varnod	Sauce/Saussy	David
	Frantions	Schetfley	John Lewis
	Jacob Henry	Schffele	Henry
	Mariane	Shille	Mr.
Michall	John	Shipard	Daniel
Michel	Levis	Sibilla	Anna
Miller	John Jacob	Spach	Jonas
Mingerodorffe	George	Sterchy	James
Mingier	Daniel		Peter
Mongui	Francis	Stranblar	John
Muron	Abraham	Stuly	Jacob
Myer	Gasper	Susanns	Anna
Neef	John	Talebach	George
Neuman	Jean Rudolph	Tanner	Jacob
Nichols	David	Terner	James
Nicolas	Son	Thermia	Anthoine
Ortellier	Daniel Jacob	Valours	Jacques
Ottalia	Janett	Vanderheyd/	
	Maria	Vannerheid	Peter J.
Overy	Isaac	Varnod	Mdme.
Pallons	Anthony	Verdier	Andre
Pelow	Jonas	Vernays	Francis
Perrotet	John Peter	Vernezobre	Daniel
Perry	John	Veuve	Anne Valleton
Piarsh	Hugett	Vigneu	Stephen
Pichard	Charles Jacob	Viller	Anna
Pinnell	Abell	Voucher	Alles
Pleir	John Rodolph	Williams	Robert
Poyas	John Lewis	Winkler	Frederick
Price	Rice		Luis
Purry	Charles		Andrew
	Rodolff		Catarina Anna
Quinch	Lewis		Jacob
Rachie	Urich		Jaque
Recorder	Francis Lewis		Jaque son
Recordon	Pierre Louis		Nicholas
Red	Jacob	Wunderlick	John
Richard	Andriane	Yanam	Francis
	James	Zouberbuker	Savastian
Riger	Michael	Zublier	David

Appendix 4

Sephardic Surnames
Coincident with Melungeon Given and Surnames [4]

Aarons	Chaves/Chavez	Gay	Luca
Abner	Coffe	Gideon	Luis
Aboab	Cohen	Goldsmith	Luna
Abraham	Costa	Gomes/Gomez	Luria
Abrams	Curel	Goren	Lyon
Aeres/Aires	Daniel	Grunwald	Mahalel
Alfahar	Dannon	Haas	Maisel
Alfaro	Daud	Hakim	Maizi
Alfonso	David	Hammer	Manasse
Alonso	Davies/Davis	Hamon	Manuel
Alva	Devalle	Hannah	Maria
Amado	Dina/Dinah	Harael	Marin
Amar	Dionis	Hart	Markes
Amir	Duran	Herman	Martins
Amon	Ellis/Elias	Hezekiah	Mayo
Angel	Elvas	Isaacs	Mazal
Arias	Ely	Israel	Medina
Arie	Emanuel	Jacob	Michael
Arrabi	Enoch	Joel	Miller
Asa	Ephraim	Jonas	Minerva
Asher	Ezekiel	Jones	Miranda
Assael	Ezra	Joseph	Morao
Baissa	Falcon	Joshua	Moreno
Barbasa	Farrar/Ferrer	Juan	Morris
Barzilia	Flores	Judah	Morro
Basia	Francisco	Lara	Moshe
Behar	Franco	Lazar	Moss
Bella	Gabriel	Lazarus	Muller
Benjamin	Gaion	Leon	Nathan
Blanca	Galegos	Lewis	Navarra
Caldeon	Galway	Lion	Nehemia
Calle	Gamil	Longo	Noah
Caro	Gaon	Lopes/Lopez	Nunes
Castel/Castiel/Castle	Gaspar	Lorenzo	Oliver

---

[4]Compiled from the lists at <http://www.sephardim.com/html/translated_ names.html>.

Oro
Parairo
Pardo
Parra, Parus, Paris/Pires
Parris
Pere
Peregrin
Pereyra
Perez/Peres
Perry
Rafael
Reis/Riess
Reisser
Reuben
Ricardo
Rico

Rivas
Rivera
Rosa
Rosetta
Ross
Roth
Rubin
Russo
Saba
Saia
Salamon
Salina
Salmon
Salome
Samuel
Sasson

Saul
Sebah
Semah
Seraf
Serena
Sharet
Sherez
Silvan
Silvera/Sylvera
Simeon
Simon
Sinai
Solomon
Stevenson
Sulema
Susan

Sylva
Tabora
Talavera/Talliaferro/
    Tolliver
Thomaz
Tomas
Uri
Valentin
Valle
Villareal
Wagner
Wolfe
Yona
Zion

Appendix 5
Germanna Colonies: Surname Listing

1714[5]

Jacob Holtzclaw, wife Margaret, sons John and Henry
John Joseph Martin, wife Maria Kathrina
John Spillman, wife Mary
Herman Fishback, wife Kathrina
John Hoffman, wife Kathrina
Joseph Coons, wife Kathrina, son John, Annalis, daughter Kathrina
John Fishback, wife Agnes
Jacob Rector, wife Elizabeth, son John
Melchior Brumback, wife Elizabeth
Tillman Weaver, mother Ann Weaver
Peter Hitt, wife Elizabeth

1714, 1717, and Later[6]

Name	Settlement	Name	Settlement
Aker	Other	Beer	Other
Albright, John Justus	Before 1725	Bender, Adam	Hebron*
Amburger/Amberger,		Benneger, Peter	Hebron*
Conrad	1717	Beyerback, Henry Frederick	Hebron*
Ashby	Other	Blankenbaker, Bathalzar	1717
Aylor/Ochler, Henry	Before 1725	Blankenbaker, Matthias	
Back, Henry	Hebron*	Blankenbaker, Nicholas	717
Back, John	Hebron*	Boehme, Daniel	Hebron*
Baker, John	Hebron*	Broyles, John	1717
Ballenger, Andrew	1717	Brumback/Brumback,	
Barier/Barlow, Christooher	1717	Melcherd	1714
Baumgardner, Frederick	Hebron*	Bungard, Jacob	Hebron*

---

[5]Of these surnames all except Rector and Weaver have Ashkenazic Jewish carriers.

[6]Most of these surnames, as well, are characteristic of Ashkenazic Jews. Exceptions would include Chistler, Christopher, Duncan, McClure, Newby, Reading, Sinclair, Souther, and Stature. "Hebron" refers to the Hebron religious congregation. I believe this was a Jewish, not Protestant, collection of worshipers.

Bungard, John	Hebron*
Burdyne, Richard	Hebron*
Bush	Other
Button, Harmon	Other
Button, John	Little Fork
Carpenter, John	Before 1725
Carpenter, William	Before 1725
Castler, Mathias	Before 1725
Chelf, Philip	Hebron*
Christler, Theobald	Hebron*
Christopher, Nicholas	Before 1725
Clore, Michael	1717
Coller, Henry	Hebron*
Cook, Michael	1717
Coons/Cuntz/Koontz, John	1714
Corber, John	Hebron*
Cornwall	Other
Crecelieus, Rudolph	Hebron*
Cress/Crest, Lawrence	Hebron*
Crible/Kriebel,	
George Frederick	Hebron*
Crigler, Jacob	1717
Crim	Later
Crumber, George	Hebron*
Darnall	Other
Deal/Diehl, Daniel	Hebron*
Deer (Hirsh), Martin	Hebron*
Delph, Conrad	Later
Duncan	Other
Everhart	Hebron*
Farrow	Other
Fick	Other
Finder, Michael	Hebron*
Finks, Mark	Hebron*
Fishback/Fishbach, Harmon	1714
Fishback/Fishbach, John	1714
Fisher, Lewis	Hebron*
Fite, Theobald	Hebron*
Flender	Other
Fleshman, Cyriachus	1717
Folg Family	Before 1725
Frank, Rev. Jacob	Hebron*
Fray, John	Hebron*
Friesenhagen	Other
Garr, Andrew	Hebron*
Graham	Other

Haeger/Hager,	
Rev. John Henry	1714
Hanback	Other
Harnsberger, John	1717
Herndon	Other
Hirsh (see Deer)	Hebron*
Hitt/Heide/Heite, Peter	1714
Hoffman/Huffman, John	1714
Holt, Michael	1717
Holtzclaw, Jacob	1714
Holtzclaw, Jacob	Hebron*
Holtzclaw, Joseph	Hebron*
Hoop, Philip	Hebron*
House, Matthew	Hebron*
Huettenhen	Other
Huffman/Hoffman, Henry	Hebron*
Huffman/Hoffman, John	Hebron*
Jacoby, John Daniel	Hebron*
Kabler/Cobbler, Christopher	Before 1725
Kabler/Cobbler, Frederick	Before 1725
Kabler/Cobbler, Nicholas	Before 1725
Kaifer, Michael	1717
Kaines/Kines, John	Hebron*
Kemper/Camper, John	1714
Kerchler, Matthias	Hebron*
Kerker, Andrew	1717
Klug, Rev. George Samuel	Later
Kuenzle/Gansler, Conrad	Hebron*
Kyner, John	Hebron*
Langenbuehl, John	Hebron*
Latham	Other
Leach	Other
Leatherer/Lederer, Paul	Later
Lehman, George	Hebron*
Lipp, Heinrich	Hebron*
Long/Lang, George	1717
Lotspeich, William	Hebron*
Lyons	Other
Manspeil, Jacob	Hebron*
Martin, John Joseph	1714
Mauck, Mathias	Hebron*
McClure	Other
Michael, Francis	Before 1725
Michael, John	Before 1725
Miller, Henry	Hebron*
Miller, Jacob	Hebron*

Motz, John	1717	Stigler, Samuel	Hebron*
Moyer, George	1717	Stinesyfer/Stonecipher, John	Hebron*
Nay/Noeh, Johannes	1734, Little Fork	Stoever, Rev. John Caspar	Hebron*
Newby	Other	Stoltz, John Michael	Hebron*
Nunnamaker, Lewis	Hebron*	Stuell	Other
Oehlschutt, Conrad	Hebron*	Swindell, Timothy	Hebron*
Ohischiagel, Johannes	Hebron*	Tanner, Robert	Before 1725
Patt	Other	Tapp	Other
Paulitz, Philip	1717	Teter, George	Hebron*
Peck, John	Hebron*	Thomas, John	1717
Prosie, Jacob	Hebron*	Troller, John	Hebron*
Racer, George	Hebron*	Tullser, Andrew	Hebron*
Railsback, John	Hebron*	Urbach, Adolpoh	Hebron*
Rector, John Jacob	1714	Utterback, Herman	1714
Reading	Other	Utz, George	1717
Rineheart, Mathias	Hebron*	VanMeter	Other
Riner, Eberhard	Hebron*	Vaught/Vogt, John Paul	Hebron*
Rodeheaver, John	Hebron*	Walke, Martin	Hebron*
Rouse, John	Before 1725	Wayland/Wieland, Thomas	Before 1725
Russell	Other	Wayman, Harman	Hebron*
Schut, Daniel	Hebron*	Wayman, Henry	Hebron*
Shafer, John	Hebron*	Weaver, Peter	1717, Hebron*
Sheible/Sheibley, George	1717	Weaver, Tillman	1714
Sinclair	Other	Weingart, Johannes	Hebron*
Slaughter, George	Hebron*	Whitescarver	Later
Slucter, Henry	1717, Hebron*	Wiley	Other
Smith, Matthew	1717	Wilholt/Wilheit, Michael	Before 1725
Smith, Michael	1717	Willer, John	Hebron*
Snyder, Henry	1717	Yager/Yeager, Nicholas	1717
Snyder, John	Hebron*	Young	Other
Snyder, Philip	Hebron*	Yowell, Christopher	Before 1725
Sohlbach	Other	Yowell, David	Before 1725
Souther, Henry	Hebron*	Yowell, John	Before 1725
Spillman, John	1714	Ziegler, Leonard	Hebron*
Spilman, Harman	Hebron*	Zimmerman, Christopher	1717
Staehr, Elizabeth	Hebron*	Zollicoffer, Jacob	Other
Stature, Rosina	Hebron*		

Appendix 6
Most Common Given Names
among First American Jewish Families[7]

Abigail	Bertha	Julia	Moses	Israel	Priscilla
Louisa	Jeanette	Deborah	George	Elvira	Golda/Goldie
Adaline	Beulah	Eleanor	Benjamin	Sophie	Naomi
Sarah	Samuel	Amanda	Charles	Lunah	Henrietta
Sipporah/		Lydia	Naphtali	Ida	Mary
Zipporah	Abraham	Eve/Eva	William	Saphira	Emanuel
Rebeccah	Solomon	Miriam	Richard	Rena	Leon
Fanny/Fannie	Jacob	Isabella	Edward	Virginia	Elias
Hannah	Isaac	Arabella	Bernard	Delia	Eugene
Bella	David	Lewis	Lavinia	Rose/Rosa	Sylvester
Melvina	Joseph	Robert	Tabitha	Lula	Nathan
Leah	Philip	Daniel	Dinah	Blanche	
Esther	John	Aaron	Inez		
Rachel	Henry	Michael	Armida		

As can be seen from these listings, several common Melungeon first names are present (e.g., Tabitha, Lavinia, Ida), yet there are some first names common among the Melungeons which were largely absent (or entirely absent) among the early Jewish families in America. Among these are Allafair, Mahalah, Jemimah, Mecca and Aliyah for women and Nimrod, Omar, Ishmael, Elkanah, Resan, and Hananiah for men. These, I believe, stem from Muslim and/or pre-1600s Hebrew-Iberian naming practices and are therefore largely unique to the Appalachian Melungeon population.

---

[7]Compiled from Malcolm H. Stern, *First American Jewish Families: 600 Genealogies, 1654–1988*, 3rd ed., updated and revised (1978; repr.: Baltimore: Ottenheimer Publishers, 1991).

Appendix 7
Analysis of Surnames and Points of Origin for First American Jewish Families[8]

Most Common Surnames

Abraham/Abrahams/Abrams
Alexander
Allen
Ancker (for Ankara, Turkey)
Andrews
Arnold
Barnet/Barnett/Barrett
Benjamin
Binswanger
Bloch/Block
Brandon
Brown/Browne
Bryan
Cardozo
Castello
Cohen/Cohn/Kohn/
Coleman/Cone
Da Vega
Da Costa
David
Davies/Davis
De Pass
De Sola
De Leon
De Lyon
De Cordova
Dreyfous/Dryefus
Elias
Emanuel
Etting
Ezekial

Falk
Fleisher
Florance
Frank/Franks
Friedman
Gans
Goldsmith
Gomez
Goodman
Goodwin
Gratz
Green/Greene
Guggenheim/Guggenheimer
Haas
Hamburger
Harby
Harris
Hart
Hays
Hecht
Hedricks/Henricks/Henriques
Heineman
Henry
Herman/Hermann
Hertz
Hess
Hirsch
Hoffman
Honywood
Horwitz
Hunt

Hyams
Hyman
Hyneman
Isaac/Isaack/Isaacs
Israel
Jackson
Jacobs/Jacoby/Jacobs
Johnson
Jonas
Jones
Joseph
Judah
Kahn
Kaufman
Kayton
Keyser
King
Kokernot
Kuhn
Kursheedt
Langner
Lawrence
Lazarus
Levi/Levy
Levin/Levine
Lewis
Lichtenstein
Lieber
Loeb
Lopes/Lopez
Lowenberg

[8]List compiled by the author from the listings in Stern, *First American Jewish Families, 600 Genealogies, 1654–1988*. Stern's compilation focuses on the origins and descendants of the 10,000 Jews who had arrived in North America by 1840.

Lyon/Lyons
Marks/Marx
Mayer/Meyer
McBlair
Mendes
Miller
Minis
Mitchell
Moise
Mordecai
Morris
Moses
Moss
Myers
Naar
Nathan/Nathans
Newman
Nicholas/Nichols
Noah
Nones
Nunes/Nunez
Nusbaum
Oppenheim/Oppenheimer
Ottolengui

Peixotto
Phillips
Pinto
Polak/Pollock/Polock
Powers
Price
Rice
Rich
Ritterband
Robinson
Rosenbaum
Rosenheim
Rosenthal
Ross
Russell
Salomon/Solomon
Salvador
Sampson/Samson
Samuel/Samuels
Schloss/Castle
Schwab
Seixas
Shaw
Sheftall

Simon/Simons
Smith
Solis
Souza
Springer
Steel
Stein
Stern
Stix
Straus/Strauss
Sulzberger
Taylor
Tobias
Valverde
Waag
Watson
Weil/Weyl/Wylie
Weinberg
Weiss
Williams
Wolf/Wolfe/Wolff/Woolf
Workum
Yates

What is remarkable about this list is how few names are what we think of today as "typically Jewish." This is because our contemporary perceptions have been biased by familiarity with the surnames found among the Ashkenazic Jewish immigrants arriving during the period 1880–1910 and during the 1930s and 1940s. Since these latter Jewish immigrants were coming from Eastern Europe and bore names such as Eiseman, Bergman, Blumberg, and as forth, we have come to perceive these as "Jewish" names.

However, Jewish arrivals in North America from the 1600–1840 period analyzed by Stern, were drawn largely from Sephardic populations who had been dwelling in Turkey, the West Indies, England, Scotland, Ireland, Germany, France, Italy, and the Netherlands prior to arriving on the North American continent. Further, once in North America, some intermarried with persons of British descent or anglicized their names, resulting in early Jewish families commonly having surnames such as Alexander, Andrews, Brown, Davis, Hunt, Jones, Jackson, Lawrence, Lyons, McBlair, Mitchell, Price, Russell, Shaw, Smith, Taylor, Williams, and Yates. However, the continuing legacy of their Iberian origins can be seen in surnames such as Cardozo, De Sola, Gomez, Peixotto, Souza, and Valverde.

It should also be noted that Stern's genealogies reveal that virtually all of the names commonly associated with Melungeons by earlier researchers were present in these early American Jewish populations, including Carter, Powers, Lee, Nichols, Collins, Hale/Hall, Green/e, Wolf(e), Wynn, etc.

Finally, it should be noted that several Sephardic Jewish names *not present* in Stern's set *were* found among early Melungeon populations, suggesting that these families likely arrived in America prior to the 1600s and/or arrived as crypto-Jews. Among these are Chaffin, Carrico, Feagin, Mowell, Houchins, Paralee, Hyatt, Falin, and Goens.

Appendix 8

Common Points of Origin and Arrival Sites For
First American Jewish Families[9]

Family	Origin	Arrival
Arons Van Blitz	Netherlands	South Carolina
Aarons	Guadeloupe	Charleston
Abraham	London	New York
Abrahams	Bremen	South Carolina
Abrahams	London	New York
Adolphus	Bonn	New York
Alexander	London	Charleston
Allen	England	Philadelphia
Ancker	England	Cincinnati
Andrews	Strasbourgh	New York
Arnold	Wurttemburg	Philadelphia
Bach	Germany	New York
Bamberger	Bavaria	Baltimore
Barnett	England	Savannah
Baruch	Poland	Camden SC
Benjamin	St. Eustatius	Charleston ?
Brickner	Bavaria	New York
Cadet	Lyons (France)	Philadelphia
Cardozo	London	New York
Carvalho	London	Philadelphia
Cohen	Swansea (Wales)	Baltimore
Cohen	Poland	Charleston
Cohen	England	Charleston
Da Costa	London	Charleston
David	Swansea (Wales)	Montreal
Davies	Holland	New York
De Cordova	Constantinople, Amsterdam, Brazil, Jamaica	Texas

[9]Compiled by the author from the lists in Stern, *First American Jewish Families, 600 Genealogies, 1654–1988.*

De Lyon	Portugal, London	Savannah
De Pass	Bourdeaux (France)	Richmond
Emanuel	Weisendorf (Germany)	Philadelphia
	Davenport (England)	
Gomez	Spain, France, Italy	New York
Harby	Morocco, England	Charleston
Hays	Holland	New York
Hendricks	Holland, London	New York

As can be seen from these examples, early American Jewish families arrived from several points in western Europe and the West Indies to diverse cities along the Eastern Seaboard. Often intermediate stops were made by the families before finally, over multiple generations, arriving in North America. It should also be noted that many of these arrivals came as *indentured servants,* meaning that they had agreed to work for a specified period of time (usually one to seven years) in return for their passage.

Appendix 9

Several additional references to religious practices among Muslims and Jews are given below which correspond to those found among the Melungeons.

Islam[10]

- Abraham's son Ishmael was believed by the prophet Mohammed to be the progenitor of the Arabic tribes. Muhammad had no sons; thus he was succeeded by caliphs chosen by his followers. These were Abu Bakr, Umar/Omar, Uthman, and Ali. Favored among Muhammad's wives and daughters were A'Ishah, Fatima, and Umm Salamah. Thus, the use of these names denotes probable Islamic ancestry. So also do names composed from the words Ummah, Haj, Basra, Kufah, Mecca, Hasan, and Medina.
- Within Islam, there is no belief in original sin, no holy trinity and no ordination of priests. Muslims do believe in free will, angels as sacred helpers, and Judgment Day. They believe in Heaven and Hell. Muslims also believe that prophetic messengers (preachers) are commonly sent by God to people from among their own ranks—no special training is required.
- Muslims begin prayer by holding their hands upward, the palms outward, at head level (identical to the Masonic "distress" signal).
- Men and women are always seated separately in the mosque.
- Washing one's feet is obligatory before every Friday prayer service.
- Muslims, as well as Jews, often cover their heads, especially during religious services.
- Islam, like Judaism, is a patriarchal religion. Women have a secondary status and are not allowed to serve a role in religious services. They are also required to dress modestly and cover their bodies and hair.
- Virtually all mosques have a basin, well, or pavilion, for ritual bathing.
- Both Islam and Judaism forbid icons in their places of worship.

---

[10]From Walter M. Weiss, *Islam: An Illustrated Historical Overview*. Crash Course series. Hauppauge NY: Barron's, 2000.

Judaism[11]

- Among Sephardic Jews, Passover often is celebrated by feetwashing of the congregants by the rabbi or cohen.
- Sephardic Jews often decorate the tombs of holy men, *tzaddik*, with flowers, beads, candles, coins, and pebbles, believing they can perform miracles from the grave.
- Certain herbs and spices are believed to have medicinal and/or magical qualities.
- Hard-boiled eggs, served with spices such as pepper, lemon, and garlic, are a favorite food. (I suspect this is where our Appalachian "deviled eggs" came from.)

---

[11]From James R. Ross, *Fragile Branches: Travels through the Jewish Diaspora.* New York: Riverhead Books, 2000.

Appendix 10
Early American Jews
with Melungeon Surnames in Melungeon Settled Areas[12]

These represent contemporaneous branches of Melungeon families who openly practiced Judaism.

Name	Locale	Page
Solomon Davis	Petersburg VA	4
Lydia Davis	Cincinnati OH	11
Wolfe Barnett	Savannah GA	16
Kate Green	Arkansas	25
Elizabeth Bond	Altoona PA	31
Russell Pirrie	Atlantic City NJ	31
John Hall	Pennsylvania	32
Saling Wolfe	Charleston	34
James Dent	Savannah	35
Isaac Minis	Charleston	35
Sarah Barrett	Charleston	35
John Gowen	Charleston	36
Alice Hale	Richmond	36
Virginia Davis	South Carolina	36
Ansley Davis	Charleston	37
Barton Wise	Charleston	39
Katheline Carter	Charleston	39
Bill Green	Dallas	43
George Butcher	Kenova WV	45
George Lyon	Petersburg VA	48
Davis family married: Green, Dale, Barbour, Haas, Scott	Petersburg VA	48/49
Jessie Gibson	Texas	52
Jerry Davis Wynn	Greenville SC	56
Ruth Moore	Greenwood SC	56
George Yountz	Greensboro NC	56
Sarah Jones	Charleston	58
Katherine Collins	Charleston	58

[12]Compiled by the author from Stern, *First American Jewish Families, 600 Genealogies, 1654–1988.*

Elizabeth Howard	Charleston	58
Henry Williams	Charleston	61
Esther Alexander	Charleston	67
Florence Lucas	Richmond	67
Ellen Hays	Baltimore	67
Benjamin Wolf	Meadville PA	71
Abraham Minis	Philadelphia	74
Helene Barnett	New Orleans	74
James Perry Davis	Lancaster PA	75
Rhoda Evans	Lancaster PA	75
William Gray Brooks	Lewistown PA	75
John Huffnagle	Lancaster PA	75
Charles Louis Boone	Charleston	80
Eugene Power	Charleston	84
Mary Cecil Gist	Lancaster PA	87
Lucius Rogers	Philadelphia	87
Sallie Vaughan	Lexington KY	88
Caroline Bryan	Lexington KY	88
Evans Caskie Ross	Lynchburg VA	90
Elizabeth Gaither	Natural Bridge VA	91
Arthur Harby	Charleston	93
Samuel Moss	New Orleans	94
Henriette Lynn	New Orleans	94
Daniel Goodman	New Orleans	94
E. J. Thompson	New Orleans	94
Elizabeth Johnson (niece of Jefferson Davis)	Martinsville GA	96
Robert Alexander Jones	Salkenatchi SC	98
Katherine Swift	Baltimore	105
Arabella D. Wise	Vincennes VA	106
John Kiefover	Lach Haven PA	106
Sara Ann Minis	Savannah	106
William Carter	Norfolk VA	107
Annie Cass	Norfolk VA	107
John Rouse	Norfolk VA	108
Jacob Henry	Beaufort SC	115
Samuel Braun	Charleston, Savannah	117
Jessie Weaver	Asheville NC	117
Dr. Carter Maguire	Asheville NC	117
Abraham Alexander	Charleston	119
Joseph Bean	Charleston	120
Susanna Jackson	Charleston	120
Adolph Haas	South Carolina	120
--------- Collins	Charleston	120
William Cabell	Philadelphia	128
James Valentine	Philadelphia	128

Clarissa Wolfe	Louisville KY	132
James Taylor	Taylorsville VA	133
Eda Carter	Virginia	133
Lucy Davis	Albany GA	133
Manis Jacobs	New Orleans	135
Morris Powers	Cincinnati	135
Jesse Draper	Atlanta	141
M. S. Greene	Norfolk VA	143
Jacob King	Richmond VA	145
Randolph Carter	San Antonio TX	146
John Barber	Gonzales TX	146
Edgar Marks	Columbia SC	151
Claude Haines Hall	Baltimore	151
Ellen Lindsay Fisher	Baltimore	155
Walter Cabell	Baltimore	155
Edwin Chase Hoyt	Baltimore	158
(grandson of Salmon P. Chase)		
Lilly Shepherd	Columbus GA	164
George Cobb	Columbus GA	164
Corinne Davis	New Orleans	165
Joseph Price	Hamburg SC	167
Thomas Paine	Milledgeville GA	168
Susan Sommers	Germantown PA	168
Alice Haile	Louisiana	168
Samuel Hamilton	Chester SC	169
Peregrine Falconer	Baltimore	170
Rebecca Powers	Louisville KY	172
Harry Wylie	Montgomery AL	173
Rudolph Wise	St. Louis	174
George Gibbs Houston	Sumter SC	176
Robert Campbell	Charleston	176
Joseph Barnett	Mayesville SC	179
Pendleton Bryan	Richmond	181
Isaac Lyons	Columbia SC	183
Elizabeth Christian	Baltimore	183
Samuel Valentine	Charleston	184
Rai Fox	Columbia SC	186
Morton Beiler	New Orleans	186
Edward Mayo	Philadelphia	187
Sara Wise	Virginia	188
(daughter of Henry Wise, governor of Virginia)		
Kate Randolph	Virginia	188
Tarris Maas	Merdian MS	189
Jeffrey Woods	Corpus Christy TX	189
Simon Minis	Savannah	194
Mabel Henry	Savannah	194

Bibliography

Adams, James Taylor, comp. *Family Burying Grounds in Wise County, Virginia.* Wise VA: Wise County Historical Society, 1980s(?). Alternate title: *Family Burying Grounds Record #1, Wise County, Virginia,* compiled in the 1930s.

Adams, Jason. "Self-Determination on the Paleface Reservation: The Melungeon Reemergence in Southern Appalachia." *The Multiracial Activist* online e-zine (April/May 2001). <http://.www.multiracial.com/readers/adams.html>. Also appears as a "guest editorial" in *Interracial Voice* online e-zine (N.d.— ©2001). <http://www.interracialvoice.com/jason.html>.

Addington, Luther Foster. *The Story of Wise County, Virginia.* Wise VA: Centennial Committee and School Board of Wise County, Virginia, 1956. Reprint: Johnson City TN: Overmountain Press, 1988.

Addington, Robert Milford. *History of Scott County, Virginia.* Kingsport TN: Kingsport Press, 1932. Reprint: Johnson City TN: Overmountain Press, 1992. Facsimile reprint: A Heritage Classic. Bowie MD: Heritage Books, 2002.

Alderman, Pat. *The Overmountain Men: Battle of King's Mountain, Cumberland Decade, State of Franklin, Southwest Territory.* Johnson City TN: Overmountain Press, 1986.

Allen, Felicity. *Jefferson Davis, Unconquerable Heart.* Shades of Blue and Gray series. Columbia: University of Missouri Press, 1999.

Allison, John. *Dropped Stitches in Tennessee History.* Nashville: Marshall & Bruce, c1897. Reprint: Johnson City TN: Overmountain Press, 1991.

Amado, Melissa I. "The Descendants of the Conversos: A Comparative Discussion of Practices." Posted on the Bloom Southwest Jewish Archives site (N.d.): <http://www.library.arizona.edu/images/swja/conpapr.htm>. "A portion of this paper was presented to the Western Jewish Studies Association Third Annual Conference held at the University of Arizona, April 6, 1997."

Angel, Marc D. *The Jews of Rhodes: The History of a Sephardic Community.* New York: Sepher-Hermon Press and Union of Sephardic Congregations, 1978; second corrected printing, 1980.

Arthur, John Preston. *A History of Watauga County, North Carolina, with Sketches of Prominent Families.* Richmond: Everett Waddey Co., 1915. Reprint: Easley SC: Southern Historical Press, 1976. Reprint with added index: Johnson City TN: Overmountain Press, 1992. Reprint: Baltimore: Genealogical Publishing Co., 2002.

Ball, Bonnie Sage. *The Melungeons: Their Origin and Kin.* "Eighth edition." Haysi VA(?): B. Ball, 1984, c1969. "Second edition." Haysi VA: B. S. Ball, 1970.

————. *The Melungeons: Notes on the Origin of a Race.* Revised edition (of *The Melungeons: Their Origin and Kin*). Illustrations by Randy Hodge. Johnson City TN: Overmountain Press, 1992.

Barnes, Robert Willian, F. Edward Wright, et al. *Colonial Families of the Eastern Shore of Maryland.* Westminster MD: Willow Bend Books and Family Line Publications, 1996– .

Benbassa, Esther, and Aron Rodrigue. *Sephardi Jewry: A History of the Judeo-Spanish Community, 14th–20th Centuries.* Reissue with new introduction of *The Jews of the Balkans* (see below). Jewish Communities in the Modern World 2. Berkeley: University of California Press, 2002.

————. *The Jews of the Balkans: The Judeo-Spanish Community, 15th to 20th Centuries.* Jewish Communities of the Modern World 2. Oxford UK and Cambridge MA: Blackwell, 1995.

Beresniak, Daniel, and Laziz Hamani. *Symbols of Freemasonry.* New York: Assouline, 2000.

Bible, Jean Patterson. *Melungeons Yesterday and Today.* Jefferson City TN: Bible, 1975. Sixth printing: Signal Mountain TN: Mountain Press, n.d. (©1975).

Brett, Michael, and Elizabeth Fentress. *The Berbers.* The Peoples of Africa. Malden MA and Oxford UK: Blackwell, 2002, 1997, 1996.

Brown, Nancy Clark, and Rhonda Robertson. *The Addingtons of Virginia: The Descendants of William Addington and Margaret Cromwell.* Alt. title: *Descendants of Willian Addington and Margaret Cromwell.* Wise VA: Sainte Marie on the Clinch, 1994.

Canelo, David Augusto. *The Last Crypto-Jews of Portugal.* Revised edition. Translated (from the first edition—see below) by Werner Talmon-l'Armee. Edited and introduced by Rabbi Joshua Stampfer. Portland OR: IJS, 1990.

————. *Os Últimos Criptojudeus em Portugal.* Second edition. Belmonte, Portugal: Câmara Municipal de Belmonte, 2001. First edition. Belmonte: Centro de Cultura Pedro Álvares Cabral, 1987.

Coeburn Kiwanis Club. *Coeburn, Virginia Area History.* Johnston City TN: Overmountain Press, 1994.

Cohen, Martin A., and Abraham J. Peck. *Sephardim in the Americas: Studies in Culture and History.* Judaic Studies Series. Tuscaloosa: University of Alabama Press, 1993. American Jewish Archives 44/1. Cincinnati: American Jewish Archives, 1992.

Dias, Eduardo Mayone. "Crypto-Jews in Portugal—A Clandestine Existence." HaLapid, Journal of the Society for Crypto-Judaic Studies (Winter 2000). Accessed 25 February 2004 at <htto://www.cryptojews.com/cryptoJews inPortugal.htm>.

_____. *Portugal's Secret Jews: The End of an Era.* Rumford RI: Peregrinaçâo Publications, 1999.

Dixon, Max. *The Wataugans.* Tennessee in the Eighteenth Century series. Nashville: Tennessee American Revolution Bicentennial Commission, 1976. Reprint: Johnson City TN: Overmountain Press, 1989.

_____. *The Wataugans, Their History and Their Influence on Southern Appalachia and the Nation.* American Revolution Roundtable. Boone NC: Appalachian Consortium Press, 1976. Edited transcript of the taped proceedings of a roundtable held 22 June 1976, at Elizabethton TN, to celebrate the issuance of *The Wataugans,* by Max Dixon (see above).

Dorgan, Howard. *Giving Glory to God in Appalachia: Worship Practices of Six Baptist Subdenominations.* Knoxville: University of Tennessee Press, 1987; repr. 1989, 1990.

_____. *The Old Regular Baptists of Central Appalachia: Brothers and Sisters in Hope.* Knoxville: University of Tennessee Press, 1989.

Doughty, Richard Harrison. *Greeneville: One Hundred Year Portrait, 1775–1875.* Kingsport TN: Kingsport Press, 1975.

Draper, Lyman Copeland. *The Life of Daniel Boone.* Edited with an introduction by Ted Franklin Belue. Mechanicsburg PA: Stackpole Books, 1998. (An edited compilation of Draper's incomplete manuscript and files which Draper set aside in 1855.)

Elder, Pat Spurlock. *Melungeons: Examining an Appalachian Legend.* Blountville TN: Continuity Press, 1999.

Embree, Elihu. *The Emancipator (Complete).* To which are added a sketch of the author by Robert H. White and two hitherto unpublished antislavery memorials. Jonesborough TN: Elihu Embree, 1820. Repr.: Nashville TN: B. H. Murphy, 1932. Repr.: Jonesborough TN: Embreeville Publications, 1995.

Esposito, John L., editor. *The Oxford History of Islam.* New York: Oxford University Press, 1999.

Fink, Paul M. *Jonesborough: The First Century of Tennessee's First Town, 1776–1876.* Johnson City TN: Overmountain Press, 1989.

Fletcher, Richard A. *Moorish Spain.* First American edition: New York: Henry Holt, 1992. Reprint: Berkeley: University of California Press, 1993. First edition: London: Weidenfeld & Nicolson, 1992. Reprint: London: Phoenix Press, 2001.

Gallegos, Eloy J. *The Melungeons: The Pioneers of the Interior Southeastern United States, 1526–1997.* Spanish Pioneers in United States History. Knoxville TN: Villagra Press, 1997.

_____. *Santa Elena: Spanish Settlements on the Atlantic Seaboard from Florida to Virginia, 1513 to 1607.* Spanish Pioneers in United States History. Knoxville TN: Villagra Press, 1998.

Gitlitz, David M. *Secrecy and Deceit: The Religion of the Crypto-Jews.* Philadelphia: Jewish Publication Society, 1996. Reprint: Jewish Latin America series. Introduction by Lian Stavans. Albuquerque: University of New Mexico Press, 2002.

Harris, Katherine. "A Short History of Florida." <http://dhr.dos.stata.fl.us/flafacts/shorthis.html>

Harris, Malcolm Hart. *History of Louisa County, Virginia.* Richmond VA: Dietz Press, 1963.

Hawkins County Genealogical and Historical Society. *Cemeteries of Hawkins County, Tennessee.* Alt. title: *Hawkins County, Tennessee Cemeteries.* Four volumes. Rogersville TN: Hawkins County Genealogical Society, 1985–1991.

Hernandez, Frances. "The Secret Jews of the Southwest." *American Jewish Archives* 44 (1992): 411-54.

Hudson, Charles M. *The Juan Pardo Expeditions: Explorations of the Carolinas and Tennessee, 1566–1568.* With documents relating to the Pardo expeditions, transcribed, translated, and annotated by Paul E. Hoffman. Washington: Smithsonian Institution Press, 1990.

Huff, Carol. "The Old Regular Baptists." *The Appalachian Quarterly* 5/4 (December 2000): 84-86.

Huhta, James K. "The Colonial Background of the History of Tennessee: A North Carolina Contribution." *The Tennessee Junior Historian* 1/1 (October 1968): 2-22.

Johnson, Charles August. *A Narrative History of Wise County, Virginia.* Introduction by James N. Hillman. New York: Norton, 1938. Repr.: Johnson City TN: Overmountain Press, 1988.

Johnson, Mattie Ruth. *My Melungeon Heritage: A Story of Life on Newman's Ridge.* Johnson City TN: Overmountain Press, 1997.

Jourdan, Elise Greenup. *Early Families of Southern Maryland.* Volume 5. Westminster MD: Family Line Publications, 1996.

_____. *Early Families of Southern Maryland.* Volume 8. Westminster MD: Willow Bend Books, 2000, 1991.

Kennedy, N. Brent, and Robyn Vaughan Kennedy. *The Melungeons: The Resurrection of a Proud People. An Untold Story of Ethnic Cleansing in America.* Macon GA: Mercer University Press, 1994. Second, revised, and corrected edition. Macon GA: Mercer University Press, 1997.

Kessel, Barbara. *Suddenly Jewish: Jews Raised as Gentiles Discover Their Jewish Roots*. Brandeis Series in Jewish History, Culture, and Life. Hanover NH: University Press of New England, 2000.

Langdon, Barbara Tracy. *The Melungeons: An Annotated Bibliography: References in Both Fiction and Nonfiction*. Woodville TX: Dogwood Press, 1998.

Lavender, Abraham D. "Huguenots and Hebrews: A Sociohistorical Explanation of Hebrew Symbols on the Huguenot Seal." *Transactions* [of the Huguenot Society of South Carolina] 98 (1993): 39-43.

_____. "Searching for Crypto-Jews in France: From Spanish Jews to French Huguenots." *HaLapid* (December 1996). Online at <http://www.cryptojews.com/HUGANOTS.html>.

Lewis, Thomas M. N., and Madeline D. Kneberg Lewis. *Tribes That Slumber: Indian Times in the Tennessee Region*. Knoxville: University of Tennessee press, 1958; 8th ptg. 1986.

Lonesome Pine Office on Youth. *Looking Back: Wise County in the Early Years*. Wise VA: Lonesome Pine Office on Youth, 1992.

Lopez y Cadena, Alberto Omero. "Our Secret Heritage: Crypto-Jews of South Texas." *HaLapid* 9/3 (Summer 2002): 1-2, 8-9.

McConnell, Catherine Sanders. *High on a Windy Hill*. Repr.: Johnson City TN: Overmountain Press, 1995. Original: Bristol TN; King Printing Co., 1968.

Malka, Jeffrey S. *Sephardic Genealogy: Discovering Your Sephardic Ancestors and Their World*. Bergenfield NJ: Avotaynu, 2002.

Marler, Don C. *Redbones of Louisiana*. Hemphill TX: Dogwood Press, 2003.

Medford, Robert Joseph, and Connie Medford, compilers. *The Families of Haywood County, North Carolina: Based on the 1810 to 1840 Census Records*. Alexander NC: WorldComm, 1999.

_____. *The Families of Haywood and Jackson Counties, North Carolina: Based on the 1850 Census Records*. Alexander NC and Nashville TN: WorldComm, 1994.

Miller, Joseph Lyon. *The Descendants of Capt. Thomas Carter of "Barford," Lancaster County, Virginia: With Genealogical Notes of Many of the Allied Families*. Second edition. Bridgewater VA: Carrier, 1912. Reprint: Harrisonburg VA: C. J. Carrier Co., 1997. (Now available on "The Carter Family CD": <http://www.rarebookreprints.com/Carterfamily.html>.)

Miller, Lee. *Roanoke: Solving the Mystery of the Lost Colony*. London: Jonathan Cape, 2000. First American edition: New York: Arcade Publishers, 2001. Reprint: New York: Penguin Books, 2002.

Naylor, Phyllis Reynolds. *Sang Spell*. A Jean Karl Book. New York: Atheneum Books for Young Readers, 1998.

Overby, DruAnna. Introduction by Katie Hoffmann Doman. *Windows on the Past: The Cultural Heritage of Vardy, Hancock County, Tennessee*. Sneedville TN: Vardy Community Historical Society, 2002.

Powell, William Stevens, James K. Huhta, and Thomas J. Farnham, compilers and editors. *The Regulators in North Carolina: A Documentary History, 1759–1776.* Raleigh NC: State Department of Archives and History, 1971.

Robinson, John J. *Born in Blood: The Lost Secrets of Freemasonry.* New York: M. Evans & Co., 1989. Reprint: Arrow, 1993.

Ross, James R. *Fragile Branches: Travels through the Jewish Diaspora.* New York: Riverhead Books, 2000; pbk. repr. 2001.

Roth, Cecil. *The Spanish Inquisition.* London: R. Hale, 1937. New York: W. W. Norton, 1994; reissued 1996.

Sams, Conway Whittle. *The Conquest of Virginia: The First Attempt; Being an Account of Sir Walter Raleigh's Colony on Roanoke Island, Based on the Original Records, and Incidents in the Life of Raleigh, 1584–1602.* Norfolk VA: Keyser-Doherty Printing Corp., 1924.

Sedycias, João. "Straddling Two Worlds: The Sephardic Presence in Northeastern Brazil." Posted (1998; ©1990) online at <http://home.yawl.com.br/hp/sedycias/sephard.htm>. "This paper was presented by the author at the Annual Convention of the Modern Language Association [MLA], Chicago, December 1990."

South, Stanley A. *Archaeology at Santa Elena: Doorway to the Past.* Columbia: University of South Carolina, South Carolina Institute of Archaeology and Anthropology, 1991.

Speed, Thomas. *The Wilderness Road: A Description of the Routes of Travel by Which the Pioneers and Early Settlers First Came to Kentucky. Prepared for the Filson Club.* Filson Club Publications 2 (variation: Kentucky Culture series). Louisville: John P. Morton & Co., 1886. Reprint: Burt Franklin Research and Source Work series 761. American Classics in History and Social Science 193. New York: Burt Franklin, 1971.

Spencer, John H. *A History of Kentucky Baptists, from 1769 to 1885, Including More than 800 Biographical Sketches.* Two volumes. Revised and corrected by Burilla B. Spencer. N.p.: J. R. Baumes, 1885. Reprint: Gallatin TN, Lafayette TN, Dayton OH: Church History Research & Archives, 1984.

Steele, Fannie Lane, and Ina Jean Stanley Dotson. *The Crabtree-Stanley Collection: A Collection of the Ancestry and Descendants of James Crabtree and James Stanley.* Midland VA: I. J. S. Dotson, 1996.

Stern, Malcolm H., compiler. *Americans of Jewish Descent.* Special Publications of the National Genealogical Society 20. Washington DC: National Genealogical Society, 1958. Reprinted from the *National Genealogical Society Quarterly* 46/2 (1958).

_____, compiler. *Americans of Jewish Descent: A Compendium of Genealogy.* Publications of the American Jewish Archives 5. Cincinnati: Hebrew Union College Press, 1960. Reprint: New York: KTAV Publishing House, 1971.

_____, compiler. *First American Jewish Families: 600 Genealogies, 1654–1977*. Cincinnati: American Jewish Archives, 1978. "Second edition" of *Americans of Jewish Descent*.

_____, compiler. *First American Jewish Families: 600 Genealogies, 1654–1988*. "Third edition, updated and revised." Baltimore: Ottenheimer Publishers, 1978; repr. 1988, 1991.

_____. "Two Studies in the Assimilation of Early American Jewry: I. Endogamic. II. Exogamic, Based on Tentatively Complete Genealogical Tables of All Jewish Families Settled in America Prior to 1840." Dissertation, Hebrew Union College–Jewish Institute of Religion, 1941(?). Microfilm of typescript: Cincinnati: American Jewish Periodical Center, 1956.

Stuart, Jesse. *Daughter of the Legend*. New York: McGraw-Hill, 1965. Reissue: Edited and with a preface by John H. Spurlock; introduction by Wilma Dykeman; afterword by N. Brent Kennedy; illustrated by Jim Marsh. Ashland KY: Stuart Foundation, 1994, 1993.

Summers, Lewis Preston. *History of Southwest Virginia, 1746–1786: Washington County, 1777–1870*. Richmond VA: J. L. Hill Printing Co., 1903. Reissue: Baltimore: for Clearfield Co. by Genealogical Publishing Co., 1995.

Sutton, Rita K. *Early Carters in Scott County, Virginia*. N.p.: R. K. Sutton, 1981, 1983.

Tarbell, Ida Minerva. *Abraham Lincoln and His Ancestors*. Bison Books edition. Introduction by Kenneth J. Winkle. Lincoln: University of Nebraska Press, 1997. Reprinted from the original edition entitled *In the Footsteps of the Lincolns*. New York: Harper & Brothers, 1924.

Weiss, Walter M. *Islam: An Illustrated Historical Overview*. Crash Course series. Hauppauge NY: Barron's, 2000.

Withers, Alexander Scott, William Powers, and William Hacker. *Chronicles of Border Warfare: or, A History of the Settlement by the Whites, of North-western Virginia: and of the Indian Wars and Massacres, in That Section of the State; with Reflections, Anecdotes, &c.* Clarksburg VA: J. Israel, 1831. Facsimile reprint: A new edition edited and annotated by Reuben Gold Thwaites with the addition of a memoir of the author [Withers] and several illustrative notes by the late Lyman Copeland Draper. Parsons WV: McClain Printing Co., 1998.

Index

(Page numbers in *italics* indicate photographs and exhibits.)